IT'S OKAY SWEETIE..... ONE DAY YOU'LL FLY FAR, FAR AWAY.....

Mira S. Hall

It's Okay Sweetie…. One Day You'll Fly Far, Far Away…..

ISBN-978-0-615-53804-4:

DEDICATION

For all victims and survivors of abuse

You are not alone

We stand together and together we can make a difference

It's Okay Sweetie.... One Day You'll Fly Far, Far Away.....

CONTENTS

It's Okay Sweetie.... One Day You'll Fly Far, Far Away.....

ACKNOWLEDGMENTS

First and foremost, I am thankful every day to my husband Rodger who stole my heart all those decades ago and continues to inspire me. I am so thankful to him for his endless love, support and patience and sharing my life on a daily basis. Here's to many more dreams together. Eternally grateful.

I am thankful for my children – Rachel and James-Andrew. You fulfilled my dream to be a mother and to learn how much one can love. I continue to learn from you both and love you more than you could imagine.

Thank you to Rachel who encouraged me to speak out.

For all of my grandchildren who bring such joy and hope into my life, who teach me to appreciate the simple things and to live in the moment. For Kraig, the best father they could ever have.

I am thankful for my friends, both old and new; thank you for your support. I am especially grateful for two special ladies - Beth Moses, an angel who supported and believed in me when I didn't. For Antonette Romanowski, who also encouraged and supported me. Thank you ladies for speaking out for me and for all that you do for victims of abuse.

For my baby brothers, Greg and Dean. Thank you for always being there Greg with your kind words of love and support. For Dean; always a very special place in my heart. Fa.

Thank you for sharing your lives with me.

It's Okay Sweetie…. One Day You'll Fly Far, Far Away…..

1

INTRODUCTION

This is one immigrant's story of physical, mental and sexual abuse. However, it is also a story of hope, survival, triumph and inspiration. It is one woman's journey from a childhood of abuse and how she learnt to survive. It is one of extraordinary determination to one day find a much better life, no matter what that took, or where in the world that led her. It is an account of someone learning to grasp hold of even the tiniest glimmer of hope oftentimes under extreme circumstances, never letting go and always believing that she deserved better, even when she doubted at times she could hang on and survive. She never gave up, knowing that she had to make this happen on her own. Eventually leaving home at sixteen and her homeland shortly thereafter on a one-way ticket and one suitcase, knowing deep in her heart she could never return. Can she beat the odds and find that better life.

It's Okay Sweetie…. One Day You'll Fly Far, Far Away…..

2

COMING TO AMERICA

Over a year had passed since I met the man of my dreams. We would spend hour after hour dreaming about our future together. We were engaged now and my fiancé would regale me with stories of life in America. We began planning this next step in our journey together; moving to America. The thought of living in America seemed so much more foreign to me than when I flew thirteen and a half thousand miles from home and found myself living in the U.K. I was excited, yet nervous of this new adventure. I knew it wouldn't be easy being a new immigrant in yet another country, but I had no doubt that it was the right choice. I had many fears, but even more dreams, and definitely even higher hopes, therefore, I couldn't wait, and this time I wasn't alone. So once again, I found myself on yet another one-way ticket to yet another strange country. So you see, my reasons for coming to America were not that complex. Mine was a dream of a better life and a love story, plain and simple.

As I sat on a seemingly endless flight across the Atlantic Ocean with my American fiancé, I very nervously contemplated the first meeting of my future in-laws. Despite assurances, I still had a few reservations and of course, many questions about America. For instance; how do Americans treat foreigners? Will I fit in with American life? But most importantly, will this new family accept this foreigner? Perhaps those people are right who had warned me (albeit ignorantly) that everyone in America has a gun and that it's only a matter of time before you are shot at walking down the street. Coming from a country where even the police did not carry guns, this was rather a daunting thought indeed. I was excited, scared, happy, sad, hopeful, confident, and dozens of other emotions all mixed up together.

We landed at JFK Airport in New York and moved as one wave through to Customs, my fiancé going into the Citizens Queue and myself into the Foreigners'. As I awaited my turn I momentarily froze upon seeing a guard with a gun. I had never seen this before and didn't move until I was forcibly nudged in the back propelling me forward yet again closer to the front of the queue. Again those warnings about guns sprang to mind. Upon presenting my passport I was duly asked how long I intended on staying in the United States. With renewed excitement I declared, "Indefinitely", thinking to myself that I had come here to marry the man I love and begin a new and better life. At this point I was informed, in no uncertain terms, that I could not possibly do that as I had the wrong kind of visa. Further discussion ensued as I tried to grasp the full meaning of all this. Before long, other officials were called out, and after several lengthy explanations, all declared the same fate. It was not possible for me to stay! I had to leave immediately.

As it began to dawn on me the full meaning and reality of this, at least as much as I was able to understand, considering the shock I was in, I felt like I'd been physically knocked between the eyes. This was soon replaced by sheer panic as I then realised I had lost sight of my fiancé. I was pulled out of line and escorted to a separate room to be questioned; alone. My fiancé was not allowed to come in with me. Did he even know where I was? We were kept separated. Needless to say, this rattled me considerably and I must have been giving all the wrong answers as before long I was being accused of trying to enter the country illegally. By now I was frightened. Why won't they let me see my fiancé? Would I ever get to see him? Was this as far as I could go? I was asked the same questions over and over, each time with more impatience and frustration being conveyed by my accusers. Why won't they believe me? How could this be happening? I'd never so much as had a parking ticket before; now I'm being told that I'm in trouble with the United States

4

Government. I knew this was serious. I was being treated as someone who has broken the law. I had a visa stamped in my passport which said it didn't expire for another three years. However, what I didn't understand was that it was good only for transiting through the United States with a ticket out. I was told I must have known this. More questions. Now I'm literally too scared to speak. This frustrated my questioners even more.

After what seemed like an interminable length of time, and out of sheer exasperation, my interrogators, who had located my fiancé finally allowed him to enter the room. A plethora of questions continued. Soon we were being told that if we really were intending on getting married as we'd claimed was the case, then we must leave the country immediately and go to Canada or Mexico and apply for a fiancé's visa. Not until that happened, could I be considered, much less granted legal entry. They could not tell us how long that process would take, but at least several months and possibly a year. We thought about this possibility until we pooled all of our financial resources and found that we only had a little over $6.00 between us. Needless to say, that option was instantly ruled out.

After more heated questioning and even more suspicion, it was decided that the next option would be to deport me. In my ignorance and fatigue I thought that might actually be a viable solution. Perhaps I thought, I could go and visit my mother. It was soon pointed out that I would not be deported to my own country, but to the last one I was in, and to complicate matters further, it was also made abundantly clear that once deported it would be highly unlikely that I would be allowed to return to this country. Once again, a dead-end; another option ruled out. How could this be happening to us? We're in love. I may not have had any material possessions; all I had were a few dollars and everything I owned was in one suitcase, half of which was taken up by a used, handmade wedding gown but I didn't care, I had dreams and I certainly had handled far greater obstacles and much more difficult challenges in

5

my life before this. I knew we would find a way. It wouldn't be easy, but giving up at this stage was not going to happen. There was a solution, and it would be found, eventually. Surely these Government Officials would eventually see reason. Why were they treating me like a criminal anyhow? My only crime as far as I was concerned was that of falling in love with an American.

The gravity and complexity of the situation slowly began to sink in as I began to feel engulfed and overwhelmed by the sheer magnitude of the problem that these officials kept driving home to us. I started feeling quite powerless to change the situation. My fiancé patiently explained, yet again, that all we wanted to do was to get through to his family home in Colorado. Hours upon hours had gone by. Exhaustion had set in. Finally it was decided that we would be allowed to continue on to Colorado contingent upon agreeing to appear in Federal Court in six days time. The appropriate legal papers were signed to that effect; a small, yet very important step. Although relieved at this news, physically and emotionally drained, we were also excited with this small victory achieved which enabled me to stay, albeit six days.

We were finally allowed to board another flight within the country. I was feeling embarrassed at the thought of meeting my future in-laws with this hanging over our heads. What problems I was creating. My hopes of a good first impression and subsequent acceptance of me were fast-fading. However, with my fiancé sitting beside me I felt renewed strength, energy and courage. I kept reminding myself that there was a solution; we just had to discover it. After-all, we were in love and it was difficult to accept that anyone, government or not, would stand in the way of that. Although naïve, I was also optimistic and continued to be hopeful for the time-being.

Six days later we duly drove the 240 miles to the Federal Court with my future in-laws in tow in order to keep the appointed court hearing with the Federal Judge the following morning. To say the very least, this was a little frightening and intimidating to be summoned to a court such as this. The trip in itself was an adventure in more ways than one. First of all, due to the length of the journey we were compelled to stay in a hotel as I had to appear first thing in the morning before the court. All four of us had to share a hotel room together This I had never done with my fiancé, nor anyone else for that matter, so the thought of doing so with my future in-laws I'd barely met, I found very embarrassing to say the least, particularly as I had to share a bed with my fiancé's mother. My fiancé then had to share a bed with his father. We lay awake most of the night staring at each other from less than three feet away as his parents snored loudly beside us, both of course wondering what tomorrow would bring and would our lives be changed forever. Perhaps our dreams of a future together were doomed after-all. "No, that's the exhaustion speaking; don't give up!" Sleep would not come. I felt like I was in a fog, being smothered and overwhelmed by the enormity of the problem. So much had happened in just a few short days.

I was in cultural shock in more ways than one, but I constantly reminded myself that I must hang on to this dream. We must have hope. We will find a way. I had not quite grasped the full extent of the issue until well into the first Hearing, at which time I was informed that a positive outcome was highly unlikely. We were sent away with instructions to appear back in court again in the afternoon. Although the outcome looked bleak, and it wasn't a definite "no", we were ecstatic that a little time had been bought, if only a few hours. Still they continued to believe that I had intentionally tried to enter the country illegally and believe me, there was no convincing them otherwise. How could this be? Eventually, a little more time was bought as I was told that I would be put on probation whilst my case was being considered further. I was happy about this, even though it meant probation. To me it also meant hope. I was fingerprinted, mug-shots taken and told to reappear in court on yet another appointed date, during which time I was told I was not allowed to work.

Now we only had about six more weeks left until our wedding. We had people arriving from overseas as well as locally. We decided that the plans must go ahead. The long-term picture was that my fiancé would be returning to school full-time and that as I had experience and was skilled in secretarial work, I would be the main income during that time. One slight hitch; I was not allowed to work. What kind of country is this that offers one financial aid in the form of Welfare such as food stamps, yet does not allow one to work? I explained that I did not want any financial help from the Government as I was perfectly capable of continuing to earn my own way; all this to no avail. I knew that it was not possible for us to carry out this plan without me working. As we were to be living well over two hundred miles from my in-laws we made trips there in search of employment regardless. Meanwhile, wedding plans were going ahead and my fiancé was making plans to begin school full-time in a matter of weeks. Other little details complicated our days. My fiancé's mother told me that in order to get a good job I would have to sit some State exams. I studied, practiced diligently and although extremely nervous, I passed these exams, thankfully. Next on the list was the interesting task of obtaining a driver's license, which proved to be a slight disaster in its own right. My logical mind told me that if America drives on the opposite side of the road than what I was used to, then it would make perfect sense that all of the road rules would then be the opposite as well; hmm, big mistake; too many exceptions. After failing the written twice I decided that it might actually be a very good idea to study. Meanwhile, the practical aspect of driving was proving a lot more of a challenge than I'd previously expected. I'd driven off the road numerous times; up into someone's garden almost hitting a tree, not to speak of many near misses with on-coming cars due to the fact of me being on the wrong side of the road. Out of complete and utter exasperation, I proclaimed that I was not going to get my driver's license after-all, at which time it was promptly pointed out that it would be extremely difficult here to get by without one. Needless to say, eventually I did get my license. How excited and proud I was. How can the Government kick me out now? I have a driver's license; my first little step in feeling like I belonged here.

Meanwhile a volley of paperwork continued with the INS. I had to appear at the Immigration Building several more times. One trek found me lined up alongside dozens and dozens of other people seeking legal residency or resolutions to their various immigration problems. I spoke with many of these people. I found a woman who swam across the river from Mexico in order to have her baby born in America in the hope that it might have a better life. I found others who had come seeking sanctuary as they'd fled abuse or persecution of various kinds. It was here that I first heard the term "wet back". I was saddened by how some of these people were being treated. I stuck out like a sore thumb. On one such visit I was the only white person and got a taste of the injustice of racial discrimination as I was treated better than most, yet in my mind I felt as though I deserved it probably the least. After-all, I'd come not fleeing terrible things; at least not persecution by my government, or countrymen. Granted, I did have my own personal reasons as to why I had to escape, but not because I didn't love my country.

My determination to make this all work grew. It was an enormous challenge, but again I resolved in my mind that the tide would soon turn in our favour and I would be allowed to remain in America. I loved this man more than anything and I was more than willing to go to the ends of the earth to be with him. Although as modern day immigrants, or prospective immigrants our stories were different, we shared a common bond; hope for a new life; a future for ourselves and our families, whatever the reasons. I was examined by the Government doctor, the first of several. My blood was taken to make sure I was not infected with some terrible disease. I had shown them my papers to prove that I'd had vaccinations for Smallpox, Cholera and Typhoid, which I'd been told was necessary in order to get my original visa. What more could I possibly be infected with? (This was before the world knew anything about aids.)

Plans were moving right along for the wedding. We had to go to a courthouse and get a license. I couldn't help but think that a lot of American life must entail going to court. Then I was told I had to have more blood tests. So this is America? I was told that I had to have yet another physical examination. Nobody explained to me that this involved a gynecological exam; something I had never heard of much less experienced. This all came as a shock and I was convinced I was being tortured. Perhaps I thought, this was a test to see just how badly I wanted to stay here. Nothing could have prepared me for such humiliation. It was at this point I almost gave up and thought that just maybe it would be best for me to leave now and go back to what I knew. I will never get used to these crazy American ways. Life was getting more complicated and I'd only been in this country a matter of weeks. I didn't understand much, except the fact that I loved someone with all of my heart. So of course, that was the deciding factor. I had enormous hope that if we just kept fighting for this, it would work out.

Along-with preparing for a wedding, I tried to adapt to everyday life. I still didn't understand very well how Americans thought and I made many mistakes and many ignorant judgments. For instance, on one occasion we pulled up in front of a business that had a sign in the window which read, "No checks here". I excitedly said to my fiancé, "Look, let's go in there, they will not check us". Not knowing that this was how Americans spelt "cheque", I ignorantly assumed that they were not going to bodily search us. In light of everything else that had transpired thus far, this did not seem an unreasonable assumption to me. Life was full of similar episodes and lessons each day. For example, I only had two sets of clothes; therefore, the first thing I had to do was to wash them upon arrival. I could not see any wash house area. I did not recognise American laundry machines. I set about washing by hand and then went outside into the garden to hang them up to dry. I walked around everywhere looking for a clothesline. I couldn't find one anywhere. I looked over all of the fences into neighbours' gardens and was astonished to find that they too had no clotheslines. What a strange place this was.

We painted my fiancé's grandfather's house in order to earn extra money before the wedding. Soon people began arriving, some from overseas. My sister was the only one who could afford to come and represent my family. She gave me away. My family had come to accept my choices, although it would be many years before I could appreciate what my mother and grandmothers felt. It was not a personal thing toward my fiancé; the main issue being that it would entail living in America, almost 10,000 miles from home. I had left home to find freedom, peace and respect, and although I missed my mother a great deal at times and various other family members, I knew there was no way realistically that I could ever go back. It would be seventeen years before I could take my husband home to meet my family.

After the wedding we moved far over the Rocky Mountains from my husband's family. Now we could get on with the business of being our own family and starting our own life; living our dream and working toward others. My husband was in school full-time and was also working part-time. I was working full-time at a very good job that I'd got illegally apparently. Life was not that simple. Everyday I was nervous that I would be "found out" as I was still not allowed to work and if that happened I would be expelled from the country. Nothing could have prepared me for the isolation I felt. Coming from a large family, and even having family when I lived in the U.K., I now lived in a place where I knew not a soul. I'd just got married to someone my mother had not even met and I was living in fear of being deported any day now. I was a nervous wreck. I couldn't

11

concentrate very well on my work. I was not doing the job I knew I was capable of.

My legal status with the U.S. Government continued to be a big issue. More court hearings, more examinations. I was still on probation. My in-laws once again accompanied my husband and me to court. They knew a Senator in their area who had even looked into my case, unfortunately stating that it was all but hopeless. Well, we weren't going to give into that. The morning hearing was not going well at all. We were told to return later in the day. There was apparently, one more person with whom we could plead my case. As we anxiously sat in this man's office listening and pleading my case; especially listening, things were not looking very positive at all. I was far too shy to really contribute that much and I was at this stage just struggling to stay hopeful. Then, all of a sudden, my father-in-law happened to notice that this man sitting before us was obviously an avid hunter judging by the trophies and other such paraphernalia he had around his office. He then, very quietly proceeded to talk about hunting, eventually inviting him over anytime to his part of the State to hunt. That was it! Just like that, everything turned around.

This very important man, who held our future in his hands, took my papers and signed them right then and there. Nobody could believe it, least of all me. I was utterly speechless to think that after everything that had transpired to date, it could now be instantly fixed with one small, simple pencil whip. Amazing!! How could one man have the power to completely change the course of my life; our lives? Now of course I had seen as a child the impact the power of men had on my life and changing its whole course, but this was different. This time it actually worked in my favour. That lesson has stayed with me always. To say we left that Federal Court House absolutely elated that day would be a gross understatement. We were nothing short of ecstatic. Ah, now could begin the formalities of obtaining a

'Green Card'; one more step closer. I was still technically on probation and still not legally allowed to work, however, the end was most definitely in sight now. That glint of hope was now this enormous light. More red tape and paperwork went back and forth and along with it, more money of course each time. It would be well over another year before I would finally receive my Permanent Residency status and have a green card to prove it.

Life was looking up as never before. Now I could finally concentrate on adjusting to this strange culture and its very interesting people. My first winter in the Rocky Mountains of Colorado brought with it one of the worst blizzards in years. I had never even seen snow before, much less lived in it. Therefore, trudging to our apartment in knee deep snow was an interesting and challenging experience indeed. Having been raised in the South Pacific I'd never been so cold in my entire life. My husband would frequently have waiting hot water drawn in the bath for me to thaw out in. Cooking was yet another interesting venture. Being raised at sea level I now had to learn to cook at high altitude. It would be at least another year before I made the exciting discovery of those wonderful American conveniences such as cake mixes and other instant foods.

After my husband finished school we headed to the west coast with all our belongings squashed into a VW bug in search of work as this is where we were assured would be plenty of jobs available. In all of the hustle and bustle of moving I had somehow neglected to register with the Post Office; something which is no longer required for non-citizens now. How could I have overlooked this? After receiving INS notice the problem was addressed and eventually rectified, thankfully. I was still nervous at the mere thought of upsetting these Immigration officials again.

A year and a half later a daughter arrived. I took her home to meet my family. Little did I know the legal problems that would ensue as a result of this journey. Before leaving the United States I had sent my passport to my country's Embassy in Washington D.C. in order that my daughter be put on to it. This they did without question. So without a second thought, off I went. It wasn't until leaving my country for the return trip that the American airline with whom I was booked stopped me and said that I would not be able to continue as I had an American citizen on a foreign passport. How could this be? I thought all of these headaches were behind me. I was informed that if they let me through knowing this that they would risk being heavily fined. After a lot of nerve-wracking negotiations, and after the plane was held up for me, I was eventually allowed to go at my own risk, although strongly advised against it as they could not guarantee that I would not be detained upon entry to the U.S. In my mind, not returning to the U.S. was not an option. With a permanent residency status and a child born in the U.S.A. how could there possibly be trouble? How wrong I was, and once again, how naive. Sure enough, I was detained and questioned and questioned some more. I was told very clearly that it was illegal to have a United States citizen on another country's passport without them being a citizen of said country. This of course was true, but in my ignorance, I had inadvertently broken the law yet again. Eventually it was all ironed out, and despite threats of separating me from my nursing infant, an agreement was reached. Also, as I could not yet become an American citizen I was fortunately able to have my daughter made a citizen of my country as well in order that no such situation repeat itself. This did solve the problem, although I would find out much later, there were easier solutions.

I became more confident in my American way of living. I still found many things strange. However, I was beginning to understand, to a degree at least, how Americans think; a very big turning point. This was definitely something that did not happen overnight, but only came with time. I perhaps even got a little overly confident in my new-found familiarity as whilst a couple of relatives were staying with us they expressed a desire to go to Mexico. As my husband had to go overseas on business I decided I would take them to Mexico by myself, along-with an infant that is. I had never heard about such things as 'do not drink the water', not to speak of any security issues. I did not even take my passport as I'd been led to believe that as long as one has an American driver's license you could get through the border no problem. How ignorant, yet again I was. Upon re-entering back across the border into the United States I told my relatives not to speak as their accents would draw attention to the fact that they were not Americans, but I assured them they had nothing to worry about as I had an American Driver's license which of course I planned on just flashing at the Customs Officials. Fortunately for us we were lucky and encountered no major problems, just a few questions raised as to where I was from. I had forgotten that I still had an accent.

It would be ten years before I would apply for my American Citizenship. Various legalities had prevented me from doing so earlier. And so it was; with my husband and children looking on, I was sworn in as a citizen of the United States of America. It had been a very long journey and although I'd learnt an awful lot through it all, it was a journey I would not want to repeat. The relief I felt in knowing that it was all over was profound.

Many more years have passed by since that young woman arrived in America with a single suitcase, her fiancé, and a very big dream. I like to think that I have contributed to the betterment of my adopted country. I have raised and educated productive members of society and now have grandchildren whom I know will do the same. My family continue to be my utmost priority, so now with the first generation of full-blooded American citizens, I finally feel like I actually am entitled to be here. I feel a very strong responsibility to ensure not only the survival, but the success of this new branch of my family tree in my adopted country. I will continue to do my best to make sure that my children and grandchildren have all the opportunities to make that happen. As far as having any regrets; I do not in any way regret coming to this country. I have learnt to love and appreciate Americans and have found most to be tolerant, friendly and generous. I have always felt accepted and grateful that I have never felt discriminated against as a foreigner. So, despite somewhat of a rocky beginning, I never gave up hope. This country has been good to me and I will never take my citizenship for granted. I realise that most Americans never have to think about that, but for me, I will never forget. Would I recommend this route to anyone else? Believe it or not I have been asked that question many times, and as recently as this writing. My answer remains the same; think very long, and very hard, and then if you still believe in your dream, hold on to it with all of your strength and might and never, never give up. ALWAYS have hope! ALWAYS dream! As far as that young American I fell in love with all those years ago, I can honestly say, I am more in love with him now than I could possibly have imagined all those years ago. That love has not only endured through thick and thin, and could fill volumes, but it grew far beyond my expectations. I could not imagine what my life would have been like without my husband. He has been a rock of unwavering support always. He is the strongest, yet gentlest man I have ever known. He is still my hero.

From time-to-time I do look back and remember that very frightened, yet brave little girl who all those decades ago never stopped hoping and dreaming of flying far, far away in search of a better life; "It's okay sweetie, one day you will fly far away; just like those seabirds, you will be free...." I am not only free, but I have been blessed beyond measure. No words could ever come close to adequately expressing just how truly grateful I am. As far as that other most frequently asked question of, "was it worth it?" Without any hesitation whatsoever, I can say, nay shout, a resounding "YES" with all my heart. I have no doubt in my heart and mind that I married the love of my life and unquestionably would do it all over again in a heartbeat.

So, despite having some very difficult obstacles and challenges along the way; namely the assault on me as an older woman, I have been extremely blessed to have had some incredible support, particularly as this forced me to finally deal with all of the years of abuse in my younger years, the pain of which I'd carried deep within my whole life. Needless to say, this all proved to be a huge set-back for me for awhile. However, the outcome has quite literally changed my life. In finally facing my past head-on and working through it, and although very painful and laborious at times, I am a much stronger person now. Those heavy burdens I carried for so very long have finally lifted. In there place I have a far greater sense of peace and freedom. I am optimistic about what the future may bring. I am incredibly thankful that I have still been able to hold on to my dreams, and even more grateful that I'm still actually living them.

However, in order for you to really understand and appreciate all of this, it is necessary to take you back to the beginning of my story.

It's Okay Sweetie…. One Day You'll Fly Far, Far Away…..

3

I LOOK AT YOUR FACE AND CRY

Sweet baby girl, I look at your face and cry. You are so innocent, so delicate, so hopeful, so easily pleased, and so full of love; so huggable. Already your personality is emerging. You love exploring and discovering, especially along the seashore and rock-pools already: the warmth of the sand on your bare-feet, the warm sea-breeze in your face, or just paddling in the water. That is your favourite and most comfortable place to be. You have a sense of wonderment and excitement in finding new treasures like starfish and trying to pull periwinkles that have suctioned themselves on to rocks, or watching pipis and cockles burrow deep in the sand, learning they can still breathe by the bubbles you see. You love watching fish swimming freely about, and the feeling of freedom as you let the waves chase you up the beach, or watching the seabirds flying overhead. You do not see this as a separate world yet, but an extension of your own. You are learning already the voices and sounds that you feel most comfortable with: Your mother cautioning you not to go too deep, or your grandmother's interest in what you've discovered; your grandfather's whistle and laugh, especially his laugh; the sounds of children playing in the water. Those familiar sounds told you that all was right with your world. The sound of your father was not among them.

I look at your face and cry. I see the face of curiosity and life is changing; a cloud is moving across it; slowly, ever so slowly. Your world is being shaken. Comfort is being replaced with uneasiness. Soon this uneasiness is replaced with fear. The sound of your father's voice sends tremors up your spine. Your look of wonderment is being replaced with confusion; not knowing when an explosion is going to erupt around you. Your grandparents are your safety net, your sense of well-being, and when they are not around, you don't know where you stand. All you know is that your world is changing. Nothing is certain, and everything is unpredictable; that, you can count on! Instead of having fun and exploring and playing as all children should, you become preoccupied with hiding. Already you have learnt that only then do you stand a chance of being safe, if only for awhile. You become proud of how well you can do this.

I look at your face and cry. Your spirit is retreating. Your sense of fun and adventure is being replaced with a new need, 'survival'. Fear is taking over your life already and smothering all feelings of peace and security. Your body aches, your spirit is wounded, but you fight so hard to keep going. You don't deserve this! Your innocence is being whittled away at, until it no longer exists. You are so huggable!

I look at your face and cry. You try so very hard to be 'good', perfect even, but you eventually realise that no matter what you do, you can never be 'good enough'. Perhaps you think, "if I become invisible..... then I'll be safe?" This becomes one of your main survival tactics. It also makes you feel very lonely, very isolated, very insignificant, and profoundly sad.

I look at your face and weep. I see the look of resignation there. You are tired in your spirit; deep in your soul; so very tired. I see you fighting hard to not give in to defeat; always on-guard; ready for anything. You don't realise your strength though. I also see determination there, defiance almost. You CAN do it! You CAN survive! You MUST! You should not have to struggle so much, but you MUST keep going. Only then can you hope to see and experience things differently.

I look at your face and cry. It would help if you knew how much goodness there was in the world. Occasionally there is a glimmer of hope. Your grandparents take you and light floods in as darkness retreats, if only for awhile. You can breathe again. You can even laugh again. This respite is just enough to show you that you can hope again, you can believe that life can be good. You can have peace. You can feel safe. You can have respect. Your life is worth living. Because you are worth it, you must keep trying.

I look at your face and cry. "Why?" you ask; because your childhood was stolen. You had to grow up long before you were ready. You had to learn the hard cold lessons of injustice far too early in life, and from the very ones who should have protected you. Your confidence was undermined and replaced with the lowest of low self-esteem. Pain was inflicted upon you, body and soul, when you should have been hugged. You were beaten down instead of lifted up; criticized and belittled instead of encouraged and built up. You were an innocent little girl who deserved to be treated with respect and gentleness and kindness. You deserved to be reassured. Instead you had to learn that the world could be safer and less cruel than your own home.

I look at your face and cry. I wonder, "Do you know how strong you really are? Do you know you have value? Do you know your true potential? Do you know you can make a difference?" Yes, I see it now. Slowly, ever so slowly, that unmistakable look of fear changing to doubt, then hope, now optimism. The cloud is lifting. I see it; it's becoming clearer. Just grab it, hold on, and never let go. You don't have to be invisible anymore. You can become strong, much stronger than you ever imagined. You can soar; you can sing. You can even dare to dream. I believe in you!

It's Okay Sweetie…. One Day You'll Fly Far, Far Away…..

4

I MOURN FOR MY FATHER…..
….WHERE DID HE GO?

I mourn for my father. Where did he go? I know I must have one, for I have been told that is so. It can't be this man who is head of my home; no, surely that cannot be.   I hear that fathers are supposed to love their children. Some even treasure them like gifts. Fathers are supposed to, above all else, protect their children, so you couldn't possibly be my father.   Instead of protecting me and hugging me, you beat me. Why? What have I possibly done to deserve such treatment? I try so hard to be good, but you don't even see me. Why are you so angry?

I mourn for my father. Where did he go? It cannot be this tyrant who hates children so. The sound of your voice induces the deepest of fear. I hear you thundering through the house; ranting, crashing, everything askew in your wake. I must hide. Quickly! Please don't find me, please!! I learn to get better at this game, but eventually I must face you. I slowly creep out with the greatest of trepidation to learn my fate. Perhaps you will forget what minor infraction has occurred, if anything. Unfortunately, you hardly ever do. I still get beaten, often 'til I'm black and blue.

I mourn for my father. Where did he go? It cannot be this monster who hates me so. Do you not see how hard I try? It seems you look for ways to dispense of all your hate and misery on your children. I want to scream so badly, "STOP, I'm only a child!", but I have learnt that would only prolong the punishment, thereby making the pain even worse. I would look at your hands; how gently they stroked a little bird. Oh how I longed to be treated like your little birds. You would talk ever so quietly and whistle to them in such a soft voice. I knew your hands could be gentle and kind, but I was not destined to experience that. For me your hands represented violence and pain; so powerful they were. One of them could back-hand me halfway across a room.

I mourn for my father. Where did he go? It cannot be this bully who hates me so.

Fathers should cherish their children; encourage and guide them; love them unconditionally; teach them positive things, not negative. Fathers should build their children up, not tear them down, suffocating the precious life out of them. You could knock me off a chair with your closed fist for absolutely no reason at all. Perhaps it is the wrong kind of look. I become paranoid about trying to make the right facial expressions; a wrong one could get me knocked to the ground, even kicked all around. I would wonder why you didn't know what that feels like. Surely if you did, you would stop.

I mourn for my father. Where did he go? It cannot be this creature who despises me so. Each day I would tell myself, "this is going to be the day that I don't get in trouble; don't get screamed at, or hit or kicked. I just know it, today's the day. I shall be extra good; extra perfect." This became a game for me, a challenge. Sadly, the outcome was all too predictable. That was the only consistency to my life. I learnt that pain comes in many forms. You taught me that from an early age. I was never sure which hurt the most; the physical blows to my small body, or the deep wounds inflicted upon my mind. Either way, the damage to my soul was far-reaching, and the wounds almost too deep to fathom.

I mourn for my father. Where did he go? Surely it can't be this man who torments me so. Being raised with grandfathers and uncles who'd all been sent to war, I used to day-dream and hope that you too would be sent off to some far-flung war; only you wouldn't come back. I remember working in the garden and pulling up the wrong plants thinking they were weeds. I saw the fire come into your eyes and felt the panic rise in my chest. I quickly looked around to make sure I was not standing by any sharp tools that might be used in the abuse. I would think to myself, "Don't you know that I'm alive? Do you not know that I'm real, and that I feel…….?" You batter me around like some limp old rag-doll. When you've exhausted all your anger, I lay there in a crumpled, lifeless heap; too afraid to get up as I might be broken and no-one will help me. I do get up; I always get up and the whole cycle repeats itself.

I mourn for my father. Where did you go? It cannot be this cruel being who tortures me so. I've often wondered what you felt when you would find me cowered under a bed, or under the hedge, or crouched hiding in the garden frozen in fear. What did you think? What sick satisfaction could you have possibly gleaned from bullying and beating a helpless child? Do you remember hurling me from the scaffolding and literally kicking me all around the ground, my lower abdomen and pelvic area taking most of the brunt for what seemed an interminable amount of time? I screamed, I begged and pleaded for you to stop. I don't think you even heard me. I glimpsed the reflection of hell in your eyes as the full force of your fury was unleashed in a steady flow, blow after blow. It took a long time to recover from that and it would be years before I was to learn the full extent of the damage you caused that day. I struggled to have children you see. I was told that the internal physical damage and scarring was so great; so that is how you sealed my fate.

I mourn for my father. Where did you go? It cannot be you who crushes me so.

I beg for your mercy, but you do not hear. I cannot respect you; I'm too full of fear. I only show you the most impeccable behaviour. Do not confuse this with respect. How can I be the recipient of such brutal abuse and then respect you. No, that will never happen.

I mourn for my father. Where did you go? I need a father to love me so. Do you remember holding me under the water for the longest time? I knew my short life had now come to an end. I stopped struggling. I knew I must be dead. Somehow I survived that; God only knows how. Perhaps you might remember the time you terrorised me with your fully charged spear-gun? You chased me all around as yet again, I begged for my life. I could give endless more examples of the abuse you rained down upon me, but to what end? I already have a thousand memories too many, and it would be pointless to waste the effort on such a seared conscience anyway. When I wasn't being subjected to your horrific abuse myself, I often had to endure watching you taunt, terrorise and abuse my siblings. What kind of father would do such things? This is why YOU ARE NOT MY FATHER, NEVER HAVE BEEN, and NEVER WILL BE!!! No, YOU MOST DEFINITELY DO NOT DESERVE THAT HONOUR!!!! You cannot possibly ever know, much less appreciate what it is like to love unconditionally; to love, or cherish, teach and guide. The true meaning of 'fatherhood' is lost on you and well and truly beyond your capabilities. This you CHOSE to prove over and over again.

I have grieved my whole life for the father I never had. It would have been far easier to have been an orphan. I do not hate you even though some would think it fully justified, and what you definitely deserve. No, I CHOOSE not hate and that is for me, not you. I pity you though. The loss has been yours. You have condemned yourself to the hell of your own choosing. Yes that's right; the bottle. You always CHOSE that far above the welfare of your children. I waited many decades for some heartfelt apology for you. It never came. I waited until I was fifty before I finally asked you two questions: "Do you ever think about how much your alcoholism has affected your entire family?" and secondly, "Do you feel bad about it?" Even then you could not admit the horrendous injustice you inflicted upon us. You still made excuses for yourself, saying how you had learnt long ago never to regret. You still have no remorse; you have no heart. So you see, you deserve your hell.

I am a survivor. Although I am damaged; I am battle-weary; and I am deeply scarred, I am a survivor. I am strong in spite of you; stronger than you could ever imagine! You may have broken my body, but you didn't break my spirit. I have worked very hard for my life and it has been a very good life despite your attempts to destroy it. I could never have lived these past decades anywhere near you. I had to live far away; far from your poisonous mind and brutal ways. I never gave up though and I can truly say that the years the locust ate are continuing to be restored, far beyond my expectations. I have been blessed to have two children whom I have loved, nurtured and treasured with my whole being. They were respected; they were protected and above all, they were loved as all children need and deserve to be. I have had the incredible honour of watching my husband, a 'real man', be the most amazing father, who has unfailingly put his family first, always; the kind of father you CHOSE never to be. Now I have four absolutely gorgeous grandchildren. They are not your great-grandchildren though. You gave up that right many decades ago, right along with your right to ever be called a father. They are a true joy. You see, our family is our greatest gift; something you could never comprehend. So you see, despite not having a father, I feel I have been most lavishly blessed.

It's Okay Sweetie…. One Day You'll Fly Far, Far Away…..

5

A LETTER TO MY MOTHER

YOU COULD DO ANYTHING….ALMOST

I have written a letter to you a thousand times in my head, never being able to finish because I never knew where to begin. I will keep trying though, because not only do you need to know how I've been affected by your actions, but I need you to know.

I remember thinking that you could do absolutely everything. You worked harder than anyone I've ever known. I don't ever remember you not being up working long before everyone else awoke. Very early on, you didn't even have a washing machine, yet somehow, you managed to always have clean clothes for us. Every night I went to sleep listening to you still working; sometimes it would be the sound of the sewing machine humming as you made our clothes, or the ironing board squeaking as you cared for our clothes. You never just 'sat', just to sit, or to hold a child. You would be knitting our cardigans or mending. You were always so busy taking care of us that you didn't have any time just to sit with us. I would long to just be held. I don't ever remember you reading me a story; you had too much to do. I just needed to be asked if I was alright, maybe even how I felt, or what I thought once in awhile. I needed to be told that everything was going to be okay. You taught me how to sew and knit, cook and clean, but more than anything, what I really needed was to feel safe.

You taught me so many useful skills; for instance, that it is possible to somehow make a meal out of nothing. Food would be scarce at times; a lot. Thankfully we grew our own vegetables sometimes, and fished, and even had eggs from the chickens; now those times, I really felt like we were rich. But those times never lasted, and too much of the time, I remember being hungry. I remember you going without food so we could eat, but somehow there would always be the best food kept for father. Then, he might just hurl it across the room if he thought it wasn't good enough. I would get in big trouble for 'stealing bread'. I would keep trying though. How many times I would sit on that kitchen floor in the darkness and ever so carefully inching that bread drawer open, little-by-little until I could squeeze my hand down inside and take some. If I was lucky enough not to get caught I would take that bread back to my bed. I never ate it all. I was careful to save some of it for when I was hungry again. Once in awhile Mr. Mottram the baker would hand a large wooden tray of baked goodies over the fence to you. On those days we may as well have been given the crown jewels as far as I was concerned. Unfortunately, one day you discovered mice droppings all through the beautiful buns and cream cakes and pies and you threw it all away and never again would we eat from the baker's tray. What you didn't know was, I went into that rubbish and saved those cakes and breads. I picked out the mice droppings. I hid that food and I ate like a queen for days. See, you also taught me resourcefulness. You had to have known that I would sit in neighbours' fruit trees and veggie gardens, eating whatever I could find; then perhaps I wouldn't be as hungry and you wouldn't feel bad if there was not enough food. Do you remember Mr. MacLean the butcher? I would detour past his shop and in return for sweeping it out he would give me little saveloys and chipolatas. Then when there was not enough food for dinner, I would not be as hungry.

Sometimes father would disappear and not come home for days. We all knew he would come back with no money. I liked it when he was gone, and I wished he'd never come back; only then we could have peace. I used to dream about there being another war so that father would have to go away. Only then could I dare to imagine a life

Mira S. Hall

without violence, a life without fear. Only then we would have enough money to buy food and he wouldn't spend it on drink. I remember you always rushing to get us into bed very early in the hopes that we would be safely tucked away by the time he got home. So I saw you try to protect us, but as you know, it didn't always matter as many times we would still be verbally and physically abused, dragged from bed for some minor infraction, or sometimes, just for absolutely nothing. How many times I got beaten for something I didn't do and on the rare occasion being brave enough to say, "I wasn't even there", or "I didn't do it", just to be told, "well, that is for next time…." So here I learnt all so clearly about injustice, and also that it doesn't pay to speak up; the punishment would always be worse. If I just shut my mouth like you did, then it would be over sooner. I would then lie in bed, and when there were no more tears, I would vow to myself that one day I would fly away and be free and independent like the sea birds I used to watch by the hour. And I would never be hungry. My body wouldn't ache from being beaten or from hunger. I would ache though for you to hold me and tell me you will make it better and take us away. Eventually I learnt that would never happen, so I would talk to myself and say, "Its okay sweetie, one day you will fly far away from here….. somewhere, somehow, I WILL be safe."

You taught me how to make scones and cakes, and many other useful and practical things, but sadly I also learnt what it feels like to not be valued or respected. My father showed me this constantly by terrorizing me verbally and physically. You showed me this constantly by keeping me in that situation. I interpreted this as my life not being worth much. I spent my whole childhood being confused by this as on the one hand I would see how capable you were at the practicalities of everyday life, yet on the other hand, I saw how you were powerless, lacking the courage to take me, us all away from such a tyrant. Yes, I do remember times when you would try to use your body as a shield between my father and me, but most of the time you were thrown aside, powerless to stop the abuse. You could have though. You could have taken us away. You should have taken us away. I never could understand why you didn't take us to your family at least. Many of them would have taken us in. I have since learnt as an adult that your parents disapproved of my father. Perhaps that answers the question. It doesn't excuse it though. Pride should never come before a child's safety.

I know that you entertained the thought of leaving. How do I know that? I was playing under the kitchen table one day; swinging on the iron bars underneath it. The tablecloth came down the sides of the table, so you didn't see me. You came into the kitchen with our neighbour, Mrs. Caldwell. I stayed very still as I thought I would get in trouble for swinging on the table. I will always remember that conversation. You talked about leaving father. I remember feeling so happy about that; then just as quickly my heart sank as you started saying, "but where would I go with six children……..?" I wanted to scream, ANYWHERE!! I would have gladly slept in a tent to be away from my father; away from that house.

One of my earliest memories is waking up and realizing that something was different and more wrong than usual with my world. I was three and a half. I noticed that I couldn't hear you moving about the house, working and making all of those sounds that started the day. I started walking all over the house, searching everywhere for you; panicked that I couldn't find you. How could you leave me? Relatives came and took away my brothers. Then I remember being passed over the garden fence with my sister. I would eventually know that you were at the midwife's. Soon you brought home two new baby brothers. Our lives changed little, except for the fact that you were even busier; two more mouths to feed. I can't imagine how hard it was for you. I have memories of you feeding one twin as you rocked the other in the canvas bassinet with your foot. I was a baby still myself, but oh how fast I had to grow up now. I wish I had a memory of you cuddling me.

The older I got, the worse the abuse. Why could you not protect me? I would hide. I had many hiding places. We made tunnels through the hedgerows, but of course we couldn't stay there forever. I am thankful though that you let us go and stay with our grandparents. Perhaps this was your way of helping to protect us; I don't know. Sometimes we would be with them for many weeks at a time. I hated coming home. I was torn though, as I missed you, but yet, I wanted to stay with them forever. Being on their little island was the only time I ever felt truly safe. Father couldn't get to me. I learnt from my grandparents that there are adults who respect children. They never screamed at me; they never beat me. My brothers and sister and I began to laugh more. They actually talked to me like I was somebody; like I had feelings, like I mattered. They taught me so many things, not just practical. Pa especially taught me that I could do things I never dared to dream. I could see the world as he had seen. He would tell me many stories of his travels; of many good people, not just relatives, that there were a lot of good people in the world. I needed to hear all of it and I couldn't get enough of it. He taught me how to appreciate the small things in life; the way the wind blew across the water and through the trees; how good the tomato plants smelt; how fortunate we were to have such fresh fish. He taught me the names of birds, fish, trees and plants. I remember going into the bush and watching him collect honey from the hive. He would go swimming with us. We would lie floating on our backs in the sea, just enjoying the sea birds diving for food, and the quietness when we would swim under the water. He taught me that girls could learn as much as boys. I can still hear his laugh. But the most important thing he showed me was that I was important enough to be listened to. You know that I was the shyest of little girls, but with my grandparents I could actually sing. I had no fear at all when I was with them. I could only 'miss the boat' back to the main island so many times. Eventually I'd have to accept the fact that I had to go home. Sadly, I didn't consider that house to be my home. It was a place where violence happened, and any little good thing that may happen was well overshadowed by the bad. My heart and true home was on that tiny island with my grandparents. How thankful I've always been to have had that safe haven; some place where I could rest and have peace, if only for a time.

One day I knew something was terribly wrong; more wrong than usual. I couldn't find you. I walked into the bathroom looking for you and saw blood everywhere. I knew my father must have finally killed you. I panicked. The next thing I knew father had grabbed me and whisked me away to a neighbour. I don't know how many of us were there, but I remember standing at our neighbour's kitchen window with a brother. We watched as you were put in the ambulance. We stood there for a very long time. We didn't talk about it. I just knew you were dead. No-one told us what had happened so I went on thinking you were dead. I didn't know where father was and I was hoping he would never come back and get us. He will probably kill us then for sure. Eventually my grandmother came and we were taken home. I loved that she was there. My father was like a different person when his mother was there. He actually treated us well and didn't beat us. I didn't understand why, but I felt a little safer. We were told that you would be coming home, and I remember being shocked that you were not dead. You did come home, and life returned to its familiar dance. It would be many years before I learnt that all of that blood was from you losing more twins.

Violence only escalated, but my avoidance skills had become more honed. Do you remember when father decided he was going to breed dogs? I remember you were not happy about it at all. When he would come up with these schemes, and there were many, it would be all the way and every spare resource had to go into it. We didn't have enough food, yet he could somehow afford to buy the best of pure-bred dogs. I remember counting 28 dogs, including puppies at one time. He primped those dogs for the show-ring. We even had to be handlers in the show-ring. I remember before school having to clean out those sheds and after school bathing and grooming dogs. Perhaps if I did a really good job, father would notice and be nicer to me. He treated those dogs far better than his children. I don't remember him kicking them, or throwing them across a room. I could never be good enough. I could never do anything good enough. I could be knocked off a chair by his back-handed fist, or thrown on the ground and kicked around, or hit the wall and crumple in a heap on the floor like a well-worn rag-doll, have my nose broken, be bruised, but those dogs were treated with respect. When I wasn't being beaten, I often watched someone else being beaten. I'm not sure which was worse. How can anyone, much less a father throw his own child down a stairwell followed by a steel can of gasoline on top of them. No wonder my brother ran away. I should have too. We all should have. I know there were people who knew of our plight, but most turned a blind eye. There were those though, who looking back now, I see understood and always welcomed us into their homes.

We all had our own 'safe houses'. Our situation was never discussed. You would have been proud of my loyalty. However, I was always welcomed in a door and oftentimes I would just sit and say nothing, just rest. Almost always I was given something to eat or drink. Sometimes I would do work as my way to pay for it. Eventually though, I'd have to leave and go home and once again, I'd have a conversation with myself….. "Its okay sweetie, one day you'll fly far, far away from all this…… one day you'll be free".

Do you remember when father decided that we all had to paint the house? Do you remember when turpentine got put in the wrong paint? I said it was me. It wasn't. Do you remember what that cost me? I was thrown from the scaffolding to the ground. Do you remember that? Do you remember him continuing to kick and kick and kick me around the ground with his boots as I screamed for help? I remember you standing there, watching. Do you remember me screaming and begging you to call the police? I had never thought of doing that before. But you did nothing; absolutely nothing. Do you remember that? Why? My body and my spirit were breaking. I realised no-one would help me, no, not even you. Perhaps you were frozen with fear. Perhaps this is when I realised that you were a victim too. I was so confused and so devastated. Do you know what I learnt that day? It struck me very clearly that I could rely on no-one but myself to change my life. I determined more than ever that one day it WILL change. I WOULD make it happen. I WOULD find the strength and courage. I WOULD find a peaceful life...... "Its okay sweetie, one day you'll fly far, far away......."

I have huge gaps. There are missing years from my childhood. When you came to visit me in America, you asked me why I left when I did. I explained to you that I could not live in that fear anymore; that I'd always been terrified of my father and that in a way I still was. Wow, even at 36 I was still afraid of him, but I know you understood. You even said that you thought I'd blanked a lot out. You were right. I was terrified that a day might come when I would give up on my dream of a better life. I was tired; so very tired. I had to leave in order to survive; my body and my spirit. I almost felt as though there was no choice. I had to live. I have a thousand memories too many, so I hope I don't remember anymore of them.

I have never for a moment regretted leaving home. If I had just one regret, it would be that I didn't leave earlier. I had to accept that I couldn't fix things anymore. I couldn't help you anymore. I wasn't responsible for anyone else's safety. I had to be only responsible for myself. What freedom that realization brought. Do you know that my first paycheck, after I took my bus fare out, I spent entirely on food. Do you remember I brought you bags from the bakery and we sat and ate it all? Even to this day, I have to have plenty of food in my pantry. It is like security to me. It wasn't enough though for me just to leave my father's house. That was only the first step. I needed to fly as far away as possible. I needed to make an entirely new life, with no influence from home. That day finally came. I flew 13 ½ thousand miles from home. I did it!!! I was free!!! I found myself at times in what others would consider unsafe, or even dangerous situations, but how could anything be worse than the danger and fear I grew up in. I'd learnt I could survive and I could do it better on my own. Eventually I met the man of my dreams, the love of my life and my best friend. Soon I was moving to yet another country. But this would be different. I was moving to America to start a new life, but this time with someone else; someone I couldn't imagine living without.

Well, it would appear that I have beaten the odds. I've come to realize and appreciate that fact more and more as time has gone on, and I never cease to be grateful for it. I married someone who loves and respects me. I couldn't have settled for anyone less. After 36 years of marriage, I still pinch myself at how fortunate I have been. So you see my dear mother, you taught me what not to look for in a man. Your example taught me not to just 'settle'. I could not have found anyone more opposite than my father. I found someone who not only values me, but someone who loves me unconditionally; someone who couldn't conceive of intentionally hurting me; someone with whom I could laugh and cry, and best of all, dream together. I wish that you could just experience what that is like, even for a week, even for a moment, to live with someone who treasures you, respects you, loves and listens; someone who doesn't tear you down or belittle. To live in a home where there is no violence. To live with a man such as I have. You deserved so much more. You deserved to feel like I do; a queen. I am living my dream.

One of my hopes was to be stronger, much stronger than you are. I am!!! And my daughter I believe, is stronger than I am. I am now seeing that I can be even stronger than I'd ever imagined. Watching my husband as a father to our children was like watching a miracle. He loved, respected and nurtured them. He loved them for who they were. I could not have wished for anything more. I got to see on a daily basis what a father should be like. I got to see that it was possible. I have been a good mother. I was not as good as you at the practical skills, but one thing I could and did do was protect my children. They grew up in a safe home. They knew they were safe.

So you see, there is no point in me being bitter. I don't hate you for not taking me away from all that. However, I wish you had found the strength to do it. Do I think you were wrong in not protecting me and allowing me to be battered around like an old shoe; HELL YES!!! But I have survived. I could have thrived though. I have had a good life in spite of my childhood. That has been due to my choices, not yours. I am still learning, and more importantly, I am getting stronger. I have hope for the future. Life is not perfect, but it is far, far more than I could possibly have imagined as that frightened little girl all those decades ago.

I wish for you that you could have found and experienced some of the peace and love that I have been fortunate enough to have. You deserved that!

6

A MESSAGE FOR MY RAPIST

The very thought of addressing this directly toward you sickens me. I could not bear to look at your face ever again. Everything about you exudes evil in its purist form. You violated me in the most degrading ways that I could possibly have imagined. During those times and for a very long time afterward, I felt completely shattered, totally worthless; as good as dead. Where my father failed to succeed in destroying me completely, you almost finished the job to where I felt so utterly hopeless in my spirit that I thought I would not be able to go on. The sense of betrayal was almost unbearable as you had masqueraded as a friend of our family, encouraging a friendship between myself and your daughter. I looked back later and could clearly see the premeditation in the ways you manipulated situations, even convincing my family that they should entrust you with my care in order that I would be able to continue to attend my school whilst they had to go away for many months. You had deliberate plans and they would be executed and nobody or nothing would stop you, least of all me, as I was nothing.

You have no clue as to how your disgusting and most vile treatment toward me affected my life. I was an innocent little girl. I was powerless. The shame I felt was all-encompassing; all-pervasive. I felt filthy to the core; spoilt, like I could never be clean again; tainted beyond recognition, inside and out. Who would ever want me, who could ever love me? I had been shown that I was not worthy of love. I only deserved abuse. The day you decided you had a right to lay a hand on me was the day my life changed forever.

These feelings and thoughts haunted my waking hours and tormented me by night. Even when sleep would finally come, it brought neither relief, nor escape, from my thoughts which overpowered me by day as the subconscious tortured me even far more by night.

To this day it is still a complete mystery to me as to how I got through school. I walked through my days in a constant state of profound sadness, barely able to function, much less concentrate, the burden of which was crushing me and destroying me as if in a vice, gradually tightening its insidious grip until I felt as though I could barely breathe. I was utterly exhausted in body and spirit. I was like the walking dead, devoid of any peace and very little hope in my present life, much less any for my future. You would follow me; always seeming to know where I was. How many times you stalked me? I could not count. How many times you forced me into your car? I could not count. Today that is called kidnapping. You locked me in rooms. You taunted me. You laughed at my body. You beat me. You continually belittled and demeaned me in every way possible. You raped me!! How many times did you assault me, over and over again? I lost count. How many times you threatened my life? I lost count. How many times you threatened to do the same to my sister? I lost count. The saddest thing was, I believed you! You treated me as though I were not human. I was merely an object; something you could batter and assault without a thought. You had no conscience. It actually became easier for me to pretend that I was a thing. The loneliness was all-consuming. I felt different from others. I felt inferior. I belonged nowhere. I became more invisible than ever. You told me it would do no good to tell my father as I already knew that he didn't care about me anyway. This perhaps was the only truth you ever told me.

I had no peace in my home. I was still being abused there also. When it was just my father abusing me, I would at least find solace walking to and from school. Now, not only would I not find any peace, but I was no longer safe walking from school even. You found me everywhere. I would think to myself, "Am I destined to be abused wherever I go?" There was very little light for me; barely detectable; almost immeasurable. It was almost impossible to see an end in sight. The despair felt completely and utterly overwhelming; the weight of which was becoming increasingly too heavy to carry.

You portrayed yourself as a Man of God. What kind of demented mind could convince himself that he had a right to treat anyone the way you treated me. You lived a lie! You were respected in the community. You told me I was nothing. You convinced me that not only would I pay dearly, but that I would probably pay with my life if I were to tell another soul, and even if I did, nobody would ever believe me above such an upstanding and godly person such as yourself. You would proudly stand up publicly, preaching; somehow possessing the utter gall by telling people how to lead their lives; the epitome of hypocrisy. Oh yes, you had charisma, some would even say charm. It would sicken me to hear and see how people respected you, yet I knew the truth, that you were the most deceitful, despicable of men; the lowest of all. You disgust me still!

I was convinced that if I could not find a way to escape my life then I knew I would probably die. Somehow I had to find a way. I didn't know how, but I would find it. I had very little energy and even less confidence. Self-esteem was practically non-existent. Somehow I had to salvage what little will I had left. It was being devoured rapidly like some malignant tumour. I was terrified that the day was fast approaching whereby I would wake up and finally there would be none left at all. If that happened, then I may as well be dead. Somehow I had to survive. I knew I must find the mental and physical energy; somehow; I MUST. I felt an urgency that time was running out for me and the only way I was going to live was if I saved myself. It served no purpose 'wishing' you to be dead. No, I had to somehow find my own strength; a strength much stronger than yours. I determined to harness what little I had left and fight the mental fight of my life.

Slowly, ever so very slowly, the smallest, the faintest flicker of hope began to once again emerge. I knew I must grab that and hang on to it with every bit of strength that I could possibly manage to muster. Just like a tiny seed, soon it began to grow, albeit, painstakingly slow. I began to really grasp that this was MY fight, and mine alone. Giving up was most definitely <u>not an option</u>. To do that would be to choose death and I had just enough hope and will that I wanted to live, but only if I could be free; completely free. The balance between despair and hope began tipping. Little-by-little my strength to go on was returning. Although mentally and physically I was working at a snail's pace, I persisted in my quest. I knew I had to somehow pass my School Certificate, a seemingly insurmountable feat. I agonised over the amount of time I had lost. I knew it was not enough just being consciously present in my classes. Sometimes I didn't even realise what class I was in. The damage to my education seemed beyond measure, completely overwhelming; far beyond repair. I had to find a way. I knew it would not be sufficient for me to just be present in body only. Oh, so much time lost. I wondered how I could possibly dig myself out of this. I hadn't lost months; I had lost years, the knowledge of which was incredibly painful. Along with my father, <u>you </u>had robbed me of those years. I looked back many years later and saw that I did actually have the potential to succeed academically, but <u>you </u>robbed me of reaching that full potential. You robbed me of so many opportunities, which passed me by, fleeting; well beyond my grasp.

Somehow I had to take back my life. In those days that proved to be impossibly difficult. There was no education about abuse. We were not told of any options or resources for help. It was <u>never</u> talked about. It was all so very secretive. There was absolutely no support that I had seen. I knew I was on my own. My previous desperate attempts in asking for help with the only person I thought to go to, our family doctor was, although met with compassion, not helpful at all. I was not really 'heard'. I was told I would probably not be believed over such a prominent man of your position, and 'did I really want to put myself through that?" I was offered valium; more of the same 'symptom reliever' I'd been offered to help me deal with my father's abuse. So what did this tell me? It served to convince me even more that here was another person who deemed me not valuable enough to help. However, it also convinced me that I had only myself to rely on if I was ever to have a hope of changing my life; I mean really turning it around, 180 degrees.

Meanwhile you continued to stalk me and torment me. I was on-guard constantly, never resting, not only at home, but now thanks to you, wherever I went. I would tell myself over and over that one day I would rest. One day I might even be valued by someone. Dare I hope; dare I dream! Although I was in a continual state of stress because of you, I also began to get a little stronger, eventually convincing myself that not only could I survive, but that I would survive, and I would be free of my abusers; forever! Although I had to change and adapt my plans frequently, weathering many set-backs, I knew I would see it eventually. I would be free!

Against all odds, I did pass my School Certificate; not well, but I did pass. I even tried to go back to school for an extra year in the hopes of passing my University Entrance Exams with high enough marks to snag a bursary. Unfortunately this too had to be cut short for several reasons. Firstly, it meant I had to continue to contend with not only your abuse, but also my father's. It had become increasingly unbearable for me to remain in my father's house. I had to get out, and get out while I was still intact, and then worry about education. Secondly, there was no way I was going to be given a scholarship. I had been robbed of too much time which I did not have the luxury of recouping quickly enough. Therefore, university was not an option for me now. No, I would have to adjust my tack yet again. I would take business classes at night. This was not my ideal, but it was a plan that could work and bring me closer to my goals; another step closer to freedom. Another step further from your vicious clutches.

I was fortunate enough to get a good job. In fact, it was a great job. It was a Government job and I did it well. I did go to night classes. Even then you would stalk me when I would be waiting for a bus or getting off one. I never knew when you would appear. All this did was force me to relocate sooner where you couldn't find me. I learnt to live on very little, and not only was I finding the freedom and peace I so desperately needed and yearned for, I relished it. I basked in its warmth and found that I was content; happy even, for the first time in many years. The dark clouds were lifting slowly, yet steadily, and in their place, the warmest, the brightest sunshine. This was medicine for my soul; balm for my still raw wounds. I was finally out of the prison of abuse, NEVER to return. I worked and lived with people who respected me; who lifted me up, not beating me down as you had done so systematically for so very long. The first stage of the healing process had begun. I was becoming stronger, much stronger. Now, not only did I believe I had a future, but a bright future. The words I would repeat to myself over and over again during those many years of abuse came back to me, resonating deep within my soul…. "It's okay sweetie, just hang on, you <u>will</u> fly away, far, far away. You will be free, just like those sea-birds." I believed that more than ever. I vowed to myself that never again would anyone, not you, not my father, not anyone, ever abuse me or tear me down; NEVER AGAIN! I was worth something. I wasn't just a 'thing'. I really did have value. One day I would find out how much. I would be worthy of love. I really did have something to offer the world. I really would have a good life; a life I could be proud of, a life of peace.

So you see, although you almost destroyed me in every conceivable way possible, I proved to be stronger than you; much stronger. But more importantly, whereas you will never be able to, I can hold my head high, knowing that I have done my best, trying always to make the right choices, never intentionally hurting anyone, regardless of my past. Not only am I not inferior to you any more, but I have moved so far beyond any realm that you could possibly reach or understand. You inflicted upon me a suffering so great that for a time it almost completely smothered the very life out of me, but in the end, it was me who rose above it and it is you who is now suffering the consequences.

By the way, I did fly away, far, far away, to the other side of the world in fact. I did realise that dream, what I worked so long and so hard for. I am free, more free than I ever dreamt possible. I live in hope now, not despair. I am loved. I am respected. I am valued. My life is bright and my future will be brighter. And you, you can go to hell!

It's Okay Sweetie…. One Day You'll Fly Far, Far Away…..

7

HELLO GOD,
DO YOU HEAR ME,
DO YOU SEE ME?

Hello God…. I have heard about you. I heard someone even say that you can do anything and that sometimes you even help people. I'm only little God. I'm not an important person, but I was wondering if you could help my father to not hit me so much. I try so hard to be good, but I still get beaten and screamed at. I get so frightened. I try to hide but it doesn't help.

Hello God…. Do you see me God? I am hiding under the hedge. I am so scared. I hear my father screaming. Do you hear me God, I'm crying? Help me not to cry so my father doesn't find me.

Hello God…. Do you see me? I'm running God and my father is chasing me with the loaded spear-gun. He is so drunk and he's going to kill me God; he said he would. If you can see me, PLEASE HELP! I'm only little God; I can't run any faster. I need to hide. Can you hear my screams God?

Hello God…. Do you see me? I'm not dead yet. I'm trying extra hard to be very good. Perhaps if I can be extra good, you might help me. My head hurts so much today. Did you see my father knock me to the floor? I don't know why God; I was being extra good. Did you see me God? Did you hear me?

Hello God…. Do you think you could help us get better food? Perhaps then my father will not throw his plate across the room because it is not the food he wants. It almost hit my mother today. Perhaps you could help us find more food too. I saw my mother go without food again tonight.

Hello God.... Do you see me? I'm hiding up a tree. I hear my father screaming and crashing things all about. Did you see him throw my brother down the stairs? Did you see him throw the petrol can after him? Do you know why God? He was being extra good too. Do you think you can make my father go away?

Hello God.... I'm getting a bit bigger now. I can run faster and hide much better, so perhaps you won't need to help me very much after-all. My father didn't come home yesterday, or today. Perhaps you finally did make him go away. If you did, please don't let him come back. I'm not frightened when he is gone.

Hello God.... Well, he came back. He didn't have any money, which makes me nervous because that means there won't be much food, or the kind he likes. Please help him to be happy. If he's happy perhaps he won't knock anyone off a chair, or throw anyone to the floor, or against the wall. I am worried about my little brother's head. My father's anger scares me so much God. I am afraid he will kill one of us.

Hello God.... Did you see us waiting outside that pub for him for hours and hours today? We didn't know how to get home. Did you see how drunk he was when he got into the car? Did you see how frightened we were to even speak? We were frozen in place. I was afraid to breathe. Is there some way you can make him stop driving with us in the car drunk? I am afraid he will kill all of us at once.

Hello God.... Can you see me? I'm here on the shed floor. I can't go in the house until I stop crying. My nose is broken; did you hear it crack God? There are many wars in the world. Do you think you could make my father go away to war God? We don't need him.

Are you there God? Can you hear me? I'm buried under the blankets. I'm so frightened. My father has come home drunk again. Can you hear his screaming God? Why does he have to scream so much at my mother? Please don't let him come through the door.

I'm still here God. Do you see the stone wall my little brothers are being made to build? Well, today they did it all wrong. My father kicked it down. My brothers' hands are so blistered and bleeding, but they have to keep working. They're only little God; too little for such man's work. Did you see my brother get the spade caught in the concrete mixer? He didn't mean to God. He is such a good boy. He is just so tired and so little. Did you see my father bash him around the head again and throw him to the ground? I am not allowed to help them God; can you?

Do you see me God? I'm hiding under the bed. My father just hurled the heavy glass ashtray at my mother. It is good she ducked so quickly as it just missed her head and went through the wall. He's on a rampage God. He's hitting or throwing anything in his way. Don't let him find me, PLEASE!

I'm getting older God. Do you think if you can't take my father away that I could go away somewhere? Far away would be good. I'm tired God, so very tired. I don't sleep much. Do you think I could go somewhere very, very quiet? I'm good. I know my father doesn't think so, but I'm good; very good. It would be nice not to have to be on guard all the time.

Hello God.... Do you see this church my father has started taking us to? There are some kind people there and also other children to play with. I wonder if they know the secrets of our family. One of the elders frightens me. Have you seen his eyes? I don't like it when he looks at me like that. Why do we have to go to this place? They talk about you a lot, but I don't understand any of it.

Are you there God? Do you hear me? My brother ran away today. I am so happy for him. Do you think you could watch him and help him find somewhere nice to live? He is tired of getting beaten and screamed at you see. He tried to be so good, but now he is so angry. I hope he finds a good home and doesn't come back.

Where are you God? The elder with the scary eyes has locked me in a room. He's touching me God. I'm so scared. Can you hear me crying? Please send someone to help me. Please make him go away, he's hurting me. God do you hear me? Do you care?

Well God, my brother tried to find a good place, but my parents were told where he was, so they went and brought him back home. I feel so sad for him. I hope you will help him before he gives up. Now he is angrier than ever. I wish someone could help him. I wish someone could help us all.

God, I'm in the shed again. Even though I have my arm in plaster from breaking it when I fell down the steps, my father decided I would be the one to hold up those very heavy boards he was using to make shelves. I tried so hard God, but the pain in my bad arm was too much and I just couldn't hold it anymore. I let it slip. Did you see how angry my father got? Did you hear him screaming at me? Did you see him smash me against the wall? My arm cracked again, just when it was starting to heal. Can you fix my arm God?

God, are you sure you can't just help me a little. I am so very tired. I just need to rest; somewhere very peaceful; somewhere very quiet. My father says I'm useless so I'm hoping he will send me away somewhere. It doesn't look like he is going to go away, so perhaps I could. I think I would like to be an orphan. I know I could take care of myself, even if you don't have time to help me. God, do you hear me? Do I matter?

God, do you see this man with the evil eyes? He says he is a Man of God. Do you know him? He tells people he knows you. God, he is hurting me again. I know I'm a lot older and bigger now, but he is too big for me to fight, so I need your help. Where are you God? He says he will kill me if I tell anyone. I believe him! God…. where are you? Do you hear me? Do you see me? I am being raped… NOW!!

Hello God…. will this ever end? It's been a long time God and I'm still being attacked. Where were you today God? Did you see my father yank me off the scaffolding, throwing me to the ground when I was helping to paint the house?   He thinks I put the turpentine in the wrong paint. Did you see him beating me and kicking me all around the ground? Did you hear me begging for help? I can hardly move now. My whole body aches and throbs with pain. I feel completely broken. I cannot even cry anymore; it's too painful. Where are you?

Well God, I am much older now. I am still being abused by this evil man who still claims to be a man of God. He stalks me wherever I go; sometimes even forcing me into his car. I am still being abused at home. I am exhausted in my mind and in my body. I have decided that I am not important enough to be helped. I know I must help myself, and I will, but I must rest for awhile. I still believe you are there God, but perhaps you don't really help people after-all.   I cannot really see how you could possibly help in everybody's lives anyway.

Hello God…. I am not angry with you for not helping; for not taking me away. Perhaps that is not the way it is meant to be. You created the world and set everything in motion, and I suppose we all have to deal with whatever we're dealt. So many have it much worse than I, and some much better. I will handle this until I can find a way to change it. I know I will have to help myself now because I know nobody else will help me. I have to find a way soon, very soon.

Hello God…. I can't take it any longer. I have to leave now. I have to get myself out. If I stay any longer, I think I will give up. If I give up, then there's really no point to my life. I don't quite know how to go about it all, but that is not important to me at the moment. I just know I have to leave now before it's too late.

God, I did it!
I'm out!
This is MY life now!
It is up to me; totally up to me.
I know I will survive.
My decisions are mine.
My mistakes will be mine.
I will have a good life.
I am a good person and I will get better.
I will put all of this behind me.
My past will not smother me.
My past will not be an excuse.
I'm struggling, but I have hope.
I know I can do this.
I'm safe.
I am as free as I can imagine, right now.
Free

8

HOPE

Why was hope so very important for me? Well, first of all I believe that without hope I would have just been going through the physical motions of life which so much of the time seemed like a perpetual struggle just for survival when I was being verbally, and especially physically abused so much. Sometimes I felt like the walking dead. Strangely though, often when I would be in the midst of some violent abuse and was in full survival mode, I somehow knew I had to hang on to hope. "It's okay sweetie, one day you will fly far away from here; you WILL be free….." Most of the time I truly believed that my life not only could, but would get better; as long as I could continue to put one foot in front of the other, pick myself up when I was knocked down, it eventually would get better. I learnt that even in the darkest moments of despair, it was important to look for even the tiniest, faintest glimmer of light. It did not matter how minute that glimmer was, just as long as I could find it.

As I got a little older I started realising that many others in the world had and did suffer far worse than myself. After-all, I was still alive wasn't I? I was still in primary school when I began to be more aware of this. I thought about it almost constantly; clinging to the belief that my life would change for the better, eventually. Now, I don't want to give the impression that there was never any good in my life. Fortunately I did have times of respite from abuse. I had some positive role models in my extended family, thankfully. I could not imagine how much worse my life would have been if I had not been able to stay with my grandparents for extended periods of time. During these times I felt like I could breathe again; have some peace; and more importantly, feel safe. One saying I will hold close to my heart always is; "As the dew is to the flowers, gentle words are to the soul." With my grandparents this certainly was true. I was spoken to with respect, always. I was not smothered there.

Life with my grandparents on their tiny island was simple and very peaceful. I loved everything about it. There was no electricity. Along with everyone else, we generated our own by using a gasoline motorbike engine which was hooked up to car batteries where the power was stored. A wire ran to the house and we were allowed to use only one light at a time. The first thing done each morning was to fill two kettles with water which were then placed on a little kerosene primus stove to boil. One was used for the ladies to wash with, the other of course for the first tea of the day which we enjoyed before breakfast with bread and butter. The next order of business would be to get the wood/coal-burning stove going. We would often then go fishing at this time, returning for breakfast with the catch of the day, which would promptly be cooked on the spot and enjoyed along with more tea and toast.

Our water was from the rain. It was collected and stored in large outdoor tanks, one of which had a pipe that ran into the kitchen, so there was an abundance of cold water. Our bathhouse and washhouse were in a separate outbuilding supplied with cold water piped from a storage tank. This then had to be heated for the long task of washing clothes which was done only once a week. Water would be poured by buckets into a copper-lined, concrete cylinder with an iron door in the bottom where a fire would be kept going to heat the water. Coal was delivered every few months to the island by barge, when all would turn out to greet it with wheelbarrows, carts, wagons and dinghies to take home their sack-loads to fill coal-bins for cooking and heating fuel.

The same concrete cylinder which was used for laundry was also used to heat water for our baths from which it was taken by the bucketful to fill the bathtub. As bathing was officially only once a week, each day we swam in the sea, rinsing out our hair with buckets of fresh rainwater. We hung our wash on clotheslines up on a little hill behind the washhouse   where I never tired of sitting and admiring the view out over the bay. There I would see very large, sprawling weather-beaten trees hanging over the beach and water. What a gorgeous sight when they were all in bloom. They covered the entire island – a rich profusion of bright red blossoms, we commonly called Christmas trees, as this is when they were typically in flower. Terns, gannets and other seabirds would dive for fish. It was watching these birds that I would dream that someday I could be free too; "It's okay sweetie, one day you'll fly far, far away......"

I loved everything about this peaceful respite with my grandparents and oh how I'd pray it would never end. Every so often my grandfather would announce that it was time to get more shells for the pathways. Off we would all set with wagons and wheelbarrows to the back side of the island where the sandy beaches had an endless supply of the most beautiful white shells imaginable. These we took home and spread upon the pathways, where in time they broke down and made it easier to walk – they were also beautiful. It was hard work, but I loved every bit of it. Our days were peaceful and although our life there was full of little adventures, we enjoyed having routine, consistency, and above-all; feeling safe.

Daily fun could also include swimming, rowing and diving races. Fishing of course was a necessity and it was the rare child who did not grow up without a fishing line in their hands, oftentimes before they could run. Fishing nets were set out and large catches were shared with family and neighbours, and often smoked for future use. We grew vegetables in the rich volcanic soil. Fresh eggs came from the chickens each day. My grandparents would enjoy long evening walks through bush tracks or along the beautiful sandy beaches. The sea was quite literally a few feet from our doorstep where oysters could be knocked off the rocks or buckets of shellfish dug up for my grandmother's most delicious fritters. There was no television for many years, therefore our grandparents taught us to play cards and board-games; my favourite being scrabble and cribbage. These evenings were peaceful indeed; no fear of our father crashing in drunk and taking out his anger on any or all of us.

No matter how busy life got, one custom will forever be embedded within, and that is the wonderfully simple custom of dropping whatever we were doing and stopping for tea. Whether we were swimming, cleaning fish, or hanging up the wash, we would hear the bell rung by our grandmother announcing afternoon tea. This wasn't always a formal affair. Sometimes it would be simple thermos flasks and sandwiches on the edge of the water, or perhaps biscuits and tea passed around the boat as we fished. Other times however, the table was beautifully set with cloths, silver and china plates laden with hot buttered scones, brandysnaps and the most delicious biscuits and cakes. Either way, it was relished. It was a time to relax, enjoy a nice chat, or listen with rapt attention as a grandparent told stories. Never was I more content. To this day I continue to hold on to that most enjoyable and peaceful custom of sitting down for a cup of tea.

Although I was always grateful for these times, sadly they never lasted and all too soon I was thrust back into the cold, harsh reality of my real world. The days of peace and respect all too quickly fading away and in their place the complicated days of fear, insecurity and violence. Oh how I longed for the comfort and safety of my grandparents' island. I would try to remember my grandfather's wise words and laugh. Those memories would help and comfort me. Oh how I craved their simple, yet peaceful life. I at least experienced that life could be very good; safe and peaceful. This fact I would remind myself of very often and it would make me that much more determined that I would live that life again; one day. However, no matter how bleak my circumstances or outlook seemed;

no matter how impossible the odds were stacked against me for a bright and positive future, I hung on to the belief that I knew it could be better.... one day. This was not any unrealistic fantasy to me. I truly believed it was possible for me. This underlying sense of hope would be like nourishment for my soul. It gave me strength to go on, even when my body would be battered and bruised and when my spirit and mind were at their lowest and taxed beyond exhaustion.

It always helped me to recognise that my lot could always be worse, much worse, and sadly it was I knew for many people. As I was nearing the end of childhood, when I thought any abuse couldn't get worse, I was raped and sexually assaulted by a trusted family friend, who also happened to be a very upstanding, well-respected man in the community. These assaults continued for a very long time. My life was constantly threatened. I was taunted and unspeakably violent assaults inflicted upon me. Nothing at all could possibly have prepared me for the effects of this abuse on my whole being. I had never seen an animal treated as badly. To be devalued and degraded like this had some very real and very major repercussions for me; the consequences of which were all invasive, carrying many major, long-term effects, permeating every part of my soul. So much of the time I felt my little glimmer of hope being smothered. As long as I was alive I knew that no matter what, I had to preserve that little glimmer. Just stay alive!! STAY ALIVE!! My sense of survival I think was always fairly strong, even when I didn't know it. All-in-all I am so grateful for that tremendous will to not only live, but to hope for a good life, eventually. To say it was not easy to continue hoping is a gross understatement. Sometimes I had to really dig down deep for it, and although it often seemed inaccessible, it was there; perhaps only a thread, almost indistinguishable, but it was there, and once again I'd grasp it like my very life depended upon it, which it actually did, hanging on to it with every bit of strength I could possibly manage.

Not only was hope a key factor in my survival, but I later realised that without it I would not have been able to go on much less be able to dream, and to not be able to dream; well, that would only be half-living. I was desperate to dare to dream. I always had a sense of knowing deep down that I did not deserve abuse, even though circumstances could be very convincing to the contrary. How can anyone, much less an innocent child ever deserve that? I learnt very early in life that fairness did not play much of a role in things. I certainly did not have the luxury of many choices as a child, least of all any say in my environmental circumstances. However, no-one could stop me hoping and dreaming. For a long time those dreams and hopes were for such basic necessities like safety. How sad it is that any child be robbed of the basic human right, to feel safe, to not live in fear. I would dream of peace; stillness; quietness; complete calm, and freedom. These were the secret hopes I would keep to myself, deep within. I shared them with no-one. They were mine, and mine alone and nobody could take them away from me. Oh they could try, but I held on to them with a vengeance. It would happen, one day. When I was alone with my thoughts of how I wanted my life to be, I never imagined being rich. In fact, I never even thought of money at all. It was never about possessions. Everything I dreamt about could not be bought. Yes, I would have a good life one day. I would be safe. Somehow it would happen. Not only would I have a good life, it would be one I would be proud of. I would be a good person. I might even be able to make a positive difference in the world.

Eventually my hopes and dreams for my life expanded. Once I got out of this cycle of seemingly endless abuse and moved out on my own, although only sixteen, my hopes really soared. I soon found out that I could more than take care of myself. I imposed my own set of rules and boundaries upon myself, the main one being, I would not allow anyone around me who didn't respect me. I would allow absolutely no abuse of any kind. I would also do my utmost to treat others with the same level of respect I expected from them. Circumstances were tough; money was short, but the sense of freedom and accomplishment far surpassed and made up for all of that. I tried not to regret the fact that I had not left earlier. To do that would have no positive benefit and would only serve to be a waste of precious energy and time. I was just grateful to now be on my own; safe. Getting by on very little was not new for me. Therefore, surviving on my own was not ever a problem. I was frugal and resourceful, but that is another story. I had a sense of pride, knowing that I was doing a good job and that I could depend totally upon myself if I worked hard enough. My life of peace was being realised. The damage to my self-esteem had been enormous to say the very least, so to see my life change, of my own choosing did wonders in boosting my confidence.

I certainly could never have foreseen in those early years of independence all of the changes and healing that would have to take place, but little-by-little, one step at a time, progress was happening and I was happy. Even if my life didn't go beyond how it was at this point, it was still much better than it had been and beyond what I thought it would be at this stage. My capacity to dream and hope for even more in my life grew. I was making the right choices. I knew all of these dreams would not happen at once, and I was okay with that. I was used to waiting. I knew as long as I was headed in the right direction, I'd seize the right opportunities as they came along, which I was convinced they would. I felt a huge sense of responsibility when it came to making the right choices, but I had learnt that I could trust myself.

I was in a constant state of flux; however, it was all positive. Sometimes it might be two steps forward and one back, but even that was okay. I did not expect perfection and I did not expect it all to happen overnight. I knew I had to hang on to that long-term dream. It was happening already, and it would continue. No matter what obstacles presented themselves I would dig for that hope, not as deep as I used to have to dig. It was no longer a glimmer, but a brighter light for my future.

I worked hard and it paid off. I was chosen to travel temporarily as a secretary and personal assistant. This was yet another very valuable turning point in my life. I was then asked if I would consider going overseas. The first couple of job opportunities, although tempting, I felt I had to turn down. The next opportunity felt right, so I seized it. Wow, this was actually happening. I was now beginning to realise my long-term goals. I would pinch myself. I really would be flying far, far away.

I was one month shy of my nineteenth birthday when I said goodbye to friends and family. I left my country on a one-way ticket to the other side of the world with one suitcase and a couple of hundred dollars in my own currency. That was of little concern to me as more importantly, I carried within me something far more valuable; enormous dreams which to me were priceless. It was all up to me now. Nothing or nobody could make me lose grip of that hope I'd carried within me for so many years.

It was one thing taking charge of my life in my own country, but would I do as well in a foreign one. I had decided that it was well worth the risks and my hopes were alive and well. I knew it would be the adventure of my life and I knew enough to realise it would not be easy and the challenges would be great, but after what I'd been through, that wasn't much of a consideration. Those kinds of challenges I could handle as they would result from my choices. As I lay back in the seat of that enormous plane with not some small mixture of trepidation and nervousness, I also was filled with great excitement at the thought of what the future may hold for me. At the same time I felt a deep sense of sadness at having to leave some of my family. As the journey went on, it hit me very powerfully that this was actually happening to me. Those long familiar reassurances came back to me then; "Its okay sweetie, one day you'll fly far, far away, just like those seabirds, you will be free." I was finally free. I was flying and my spirit was soaring.

At this stage in my life I certainly did not equate hard times with failure. I expected some and they were certainly delivered. The best thing I did for myself was to realise that everything takes time and not much could or should be rushed. Hard times were a foregone conclusion and never any reason to abandon hopes and dreams. I eventually came to believe that I could even dream of one day having someone in my life, someone with whom I could have total trust, respect and unconditional love. However, I was not ready to take that risk any time soon. In fact, I had determined that I would not allow anything of the sort to happen until I was perhaps thirty. Hmm...... just when I thought I had it all sorted out, life threw me a curve-ball, and it came fast, and when I least expected. I could not have planned it any better myself. Along came that person. I had many reservations and at least as many fears, but deep within, I knew it was right. I could not imagine loving anyone or being loved more than this. Could this be? Could this really be the person I dared to dream about sharing my life with? I did trust this person. We respected and trusted each other, and loved each other unconditionally; much more than I could possibly have imagined. From the very beginning we dreamed together and we dream together now. We are more in love now than ever. Thirty six years later I still trust this man implicitly. I have been truly blessed with so much more than I ever hoped for. Many times I have asked myself; "what did I possibly do to deserve all this?" I can't really say, but all I know is this; I dared to hope, I dared to dream, and I am still living that dream. We are living it. Words could never do justice in explaining the depth of just how truly grateful I am to this man and the life he has given me; the life we have built together. Eternally grateful!

It's Okay Sweetie.... One Day You'll Fly Far, Far Away.....

9

FORGIVENESS

I have asked myself down through the decades, "Is it possible to forgive, I mean really and truly forgive the man who called himself my father, yet physically and mentally abused me for my entire childhood?" Is it also possible to forgive that other despicable man who raped me as a child, stalking and kidnapping me, constantly threatening my life and continuing to sexually assault me time after endless time? Is it also possible to forgive a doctor with whom I put my whole trust in and yet assaulted me as a grown woman? These 'men' who treated me like I was nothing; is it possible? These men who neither thought, nor cared about the consequences these life-long wounds they were inflicting upon me would have. Is it possible? I was disposable to them. I mattered nothing to them. I was nothing to them. Is it possible to truly forgive men such as these?

In my early twenties as I was grappling to make sense of my abuse and my abusers, I was under the strong impression that in order for me to live a meaningful, happy, and peaceful life and to truly put my past behind me that I must at least find it in my heart to forgive my father. I knew I could never respect him, but I felt an overwhelming pressure that I was required somehow to forgive him. I'm not really sure how, nor why I had formed this notion, other than perhaps it was supposed to be 'the right thing to do' and anything less would negatively affect me even more than the abuse already had. How that could be, I couldn't quite imagine. So just in case, I wasn't taking any chances, thereby, I did voice out loud my forgiveness. I believe I was sincere and even convinced myself, for awhile at least, that yes indeed, I had forgiven him. I do think however, that I was realistic enough to know that I would not suddenly 'feel good' toward him, neither would I harbour any expectations of warm or compassionate thoughts toward him. I did however, finally realise that forgiveness was probably more than just a one-time decision, and more likely some longer, possibly more complex and probably more ongoing process that I may never fully resolve. I then began to doubt that I truly had forgiven. Decades later I asked myself, "Is it even necessary for my well-being to forgive such people, all of whom committed the most disgusting, demeaning, and humiliating acts upon me, two of whom stole not only my innocence, but my childhood?" Should I be expected to forgive such people? I have been able to forgive any other hurts, but I came to believe that there are times when it is almost impossible and should not be required, much less imposed upon any victim.

Some might think that in order to not be completely consumed by bitterness, anger or resentment, it is necessary for the mind and heart to fully forgive. I no longer believe this. I believe that there are some things in this world that are unforgiveable. I have neither demanded, nor expected compensation. I don't deny that justice, or some sort of accountability would have made a tremendous difference to me, or at the very least, seeing my perpetrators taking full responsibility for what they had inflicted upon me. I think, although extremely difficult, it is possible for some to forgive under such circumstances. I have nothing but the greatest admiration for those who can do this. I must admit however, that if I were to be asked sincerely for forgiveness, and after seeing genuine remorse I too might, although with enormous difficulty, also be able to arrive at such a state; to what degree, I don't know. Unfortunately, any opportunities I have presented, even to my father have sadly been rebuffed.

I think that asking to be forgiven on the part of the perpetrator is not a prerequisite in order for forgiveness to take place. However, for some, including me, it could make the world of difference. I do believe that it is possible to not forgive and yet not hang on to resentment, holding grudges where bitterness becomes inevitable. I know I don't hate. I refuse to allow myself to hate. This I do for myself as one of my greatest fears has been that bitterness would take hold. I am determined that I would not join the myriad of people I have seen who have become terminally consumed by this. I believe that few things weaken the soul more than allowing anger and bitterness to take hold and fester, not to speak of the incredible waste of energy, emotions and effort which could not help but to permeate other areas of my life, thereby grossly impacting my own family negatively also. Therefore, I believe that gradually, over the years I have been able to relinquish, as much as possible, the importance I once gave it and the hold this once had on me. I do not refuse to forgive, however, I have become more and more convinced that not only is it not necessary for my own personal sense of well-being to offer forgiveness to all of these perpetrators, but that I don't actually believe my mental, physical or spiritual well-being would be in jeopardy in any way if there were not forgiveness.

So many people put a tremendous amount of undue pressure upon themselves to forgive, thinking that it is required in order for true healing to take place. This pressure to forgive one's abuser(s) is all too commonly imposed upon victims by well-meaning people who don't necessarily understand what it is like to be a victim of such extreme abuse. It is all too common for a victim to feel guilty or worse yet, a failure if they don't or can't forgive. After-all, I think most would agree, doesn't one usually have to earn the trust of another? Isn't respect also something that must be earned? If this is so, why then should forgiveness be excluded? Obviously this would depend upon the person and their own circumstances, but for me personally, I will no longer be freely offering my forgiveness to my abusers, not that any has been asked for by either of them. This should not be an automatic right or assumption of any such perpetrator. Some may think that by saying forgiveness must be earned implies that such abuse could be assessed some kind of measurable value. Hmm…. All I know is that the possibility of any genuine forgiveness on my part could only be realised by the actions on the part of my abusers, not just mere words. In reality though, the likelihood of any of my abusers receiving any pardon or forgiveness from me remain highly improbable.

Whilst I do not feel any need for revenge toward my father, I must admit that I have felt a profound sense of sadness and grief for what could have been, but I also know that I would feel this with or without forgiveness on my part. I think however, that I have finally relinquished the hope that the past could ever be any different. I have let go of that, along-with any need to avenge. As I began to take back the power that I had given to my offenders, I no longer feel as bound to the horrendous acts of abuse against me that I once felt and worked so hard to keep buried. Again, I have always tried to and will continue to make a concerted effort in not allowing how I've been hurt to define my life, who I am, or to use it as an excuse for how I lead my life. I haven't always been successful, but I will never give up in trying my best. I learnt long ago, that it doesn't happen by wishing, and no-one else can do it for me. The progress isn't always as fast as I'd like, but little-by-little I see it, and as long as I can see it, I have hope. Although I cannot deny that it has all affected me very deeply, I do see my strength growing. I have tried to use it to help myself become a better person, more compassionate, understanding and kind toward others. After-all, one never knows the stories or hurts another carries and at what point along their journey they are.

Although I never expected to feel totally wonderful and completely set free when I 'voiced' my forgiveness toward my father, I perhaps thought, albeit subconsciously, and perhaps naively that it might take the pain away, or at least greatly diminish it; perhaps even heal my soul faster, or dare I say it, help me to forget. Although I think that it would be ideal to be able to forgive, I'm no longer as concerned about how I would feel about myself if I don't. Being able to relieve myself of any guilt and pressure I had imposed upon myself over the years for not being able to truly forgive, has lifted an enormous burden from my heart and mind. On the other hand, I think I have possibly devoted far too much time and effort into trying to understand my abuse, and particularly my abusers logically, as well as perhaps giving too much emphasis and credence to forgiveness that I have neglected other areas of my healing process and recovery.

I feel extremely fortunate that I have been able to make healthy life choices. I had to devise my own set of standards, rules and boundaries if I ever were to have any hope of living the kind of life I not only wanted, but desperately needed. It did not have to be a perfect life, but one in which I would never settle for any type of abuse. I would only choose a life where I would be respected. Anything less would have most definitely not been an acceptable option. I would live alone before I would compromise those standards. What choice did I have if I was not to remain a victim? At times I have actually felt proud of myself for making a good life despite a rocky beginning. I must admit though that I was severely derailed for a while: shaken to the core even, when after decades of living the life of my dreams I became a victim of assault yet again as a much older woman. How could this have happened? I had vowed to myself decades earlier that no-one would ever abuse me again. I took every precaution to make sure I would never again be that kind of victim. It was almost impossible to bear that it did actually happen again. In a way, I felt like I'd failed myself. I'd taken such care to ensure that no such abuse would be inflicted upon me as in the past. This was extremely hard for me to accept. Sadly, we cannot always control such circumstances. Thankfully, I have gradually returned to the point where I no longer feel completely consumed by this or my past injuries to my mind and body. Are the wounds still there? Absolutely! And they are still very deep and in various stages of healing. Some have healed over the best that I can hope for; others are still a little more raw, open wounds, some oozing more than others. Many have different thicknesses of scabs which tend to break open at times, even resurfacing, but I have hope that gradually they too will heal. I know now that the effects of these wounds do not have to be a life sentence. Do I ever expect to forget? No, I don't believe that is possible at all. That would be forgetting or denying my entire childhood.

As I began to get stronger I became aware that the fears that had once consumed me of things being inflicted upon me again are gradually subsiding. Hope is returning. I used to think that was due to me finally beginning to grasp the true meaning of forgiveness and all that it encompasses. Now I am thinking that it is more due to the fact that I am actually becoming the strong person that I'd always dreamt of becoming. It's finally sinking in that I deserve that, and why not, I've sure worked hard for it. As I have tried to live my adult life in hope and peace, I know my future will just get brighter and brighter. I will continue to get stronger and stronger, perhaps even to the point where I can help or perhaps bring hope to others. That is one of my ultimate goals, my dream; to see something good come out of such evil.

I am still not completely without conflict as to how one can forgive without minimizing, or excusing to a certain degree what was inflicted upon them, particularly when it involves extreme abuse. Again, although I know it is possible for some people, I still find it difficult to imagine being fully in that place. For me, I will continue trying to improve myself, diligently trying not to allow the negative parts of my past to pervade my future. This is my responsibility, not only for my sake, but also for my children and future generations. I must never give up and I must always have hope!

I tried to understand for many years how anyone, much less a father, could treat a child so. I would try to convince myself that these abuses were not about me or personal in anyway, but rather the results of some inner demons of rage tormenting this abuser. This would help only rarely, and was always short-lived. I needed so desperately to make some kind of sense out of it. No matter how I tried, I could never understand what would drive anyone to that magnitude of abuse. No, I finally realised that I would never understand it. There is no logic. I could not even during those times seem to be able to excuse the behaviour in any way, and I know I never will. There are no excuses, absolutely none!

I have heard it said that there is nothing in the end which cannot be forgiven, but there remains much that is inexcusable. I tried very hard to adopt this and relate to it. The first part I worked on for so many years, but where it pertains to abuse, I have never been able to accept it. This has all been an extremely difficult and uncomfortable process. I tried for many years to remember and put into practice those wise words of Martin Luther King when he said, "Forgiveness is not an occasional act, it is a permanent attitude." However, after endless mulling over, in all honesty, do I think that forgiveness on my part will be the end result? Although I'm very doubtful, although not for lack of trying, I am prepared for the possibility of it not happening at all, and meanwhile I will not be putting any pressure on myself and most definitely will not feel a failure if it doesn't eventuate. For me to arrive at such a conclusion and truly believe it is a completely new kind of freedom. I am so grateful to be in this place.

It's Okay Sweetie…. One Day You'll Fly Far, Far Away…..

10

CONFRONTATION AND CLOSURE

I knew this day must finally come in order for me to fully take back the power which my father had wrenched from me as a child and which I'd allowed him to keep for so very long. Confrontation to me has always been synonymous with conflict, which has been something I have run from for as long as I can remember. Why is it that the very word even denotes something so very negative, powerful even and all too often thought of as something wrong? Well, I have come to realise that not only can confrontation be very right, but oftentimes, very necessary. For too many decades the very thought of confronting my father with what he had done to me and really telling him what I thought would induce such stress and fear of such mega proportions as to almost make me physically sick. Although I had wanted for many decades to finally confront him, I'd gotten to the point where I'd all but given up actually doing it, making many excuses to myself as to the necessity of it all. "What would be gained?" "No point!" "Nothing good could possibly come out of it?" "Let sleeping dogs lay." "I've survived this long without it haven't I?" "He's not going to change now, so why bother." "He's an old man now," etc. etc. After-all, I was at least dealing with my past wasn't I? However, it haunted me more and more. I knew I'd just have to face it head on, no matter what.

As I'd gotten deeper into the healing process and wading through the quagmire and muck of it all, the idea of confrontation began to trespass all too frequently on my thoughts. I knew the days I could put it off were numbered. Now I'm not saying that it is necessary for everyone to do this in order for progress to continue or healing to fully take place. There are many who simply do not have the opportunity to, perhaps due to death or some other circumstances out of their control. For me personally though, I knew it would gnaw at me until I finally took the plunge and acted on it, regardless of my feelings. Believe me, that wasn't something I relished the thought of. After-all, I was still in the midst of the very arduous, messy and painful process of confronting my past, along-with all its ugliness and fears which had a habit of rearing themselves into the forefront of my mind oftentimes without warning. I would still try to convince myself right up to the last minute that this stage of healing would not stagnate if I were to abandon all thoughts of confrontation. I was definitely seeing progress and healing. Surely I could just let go of the thought of feeling that this last step was necessary.

I have come to a new and much greater understanding and appreciation for how the mind works, and especially how mine does. I don't think I could ever begin to fathom just how complex our human thought processes can be; and how very subtly our subconscious minds can be influenced. My father had given me two things my entire life; one being a doll. As children, my siblings and I had very little in the way of possessions. I had four books that I can remember over my childhood and a couple of dolls of my own as well as a doll buggy which I shared with my sister. When I was very small my father came home with one of these dolls and gave it to me. Despite this lack of personal possessions, strangely I was never able to connect at all with this doll. Perhaps it was because of the negative feelings I had picked up on associated with this particular homecoming of my father. Very often he would disappear for days and come home with no money, which to me meant, little or no food. Of course his homecomings also meant shattered peace. This would have been an expensive doll back then and I have always wondered, with not a small amount of suspicion as to how he had come by it. I never even named it.

On one of my trips back to visit family as an adult I was given back this doll. I brought it back across an ocean and a continent. I moved it around from State–to-State. I kept it put away for the most part. Every so often I would come across it and every time it was associated with bad connotations. One day as I was in the midst of facing my past head-on I happened across this doll yet again. I pulled that doll out and sat it in a chair in the hub of the house and forced myself to look at it for a week. Even the doll looked unbearably sad. What was it about this doll? Then it finally hit me; why was I hanging on to this? It was a physical reminder of my father and each time I looked at it I felt a renewed sense of sadness and grief which inevitably brought with it a flood of overwhelmingly bad memories and emotions. After almost fifty years with this doll I realised, it had to go. With its departure came a sense of an enormous weight being lifted from me; a freedom of sorts. Interestingly enough it seemed that my father already had less of an influence on me. I felt a much greater sense of strength and boldness. Within days I picked up that phone and called the other side of the world to confront my father. I had shoved all this so far down inside of me for far too long. My eyes had been opened as to the enormity of the negative impact this had always had on my life. As I'd always been so careful and conscientious about keeping it so buried, openly this was not obvious, but deep inside I always struggled. Oftentimes I was unaware of all the ways it influenced me; especially in my perception of myself. It ate away at me; its insidiously deep roots being all-invasive and long-reaching.

Normally my father would answer the telephone if he was in the house, but I kept getting my mother. I explained to my mother all of what I felt about my childhood. Why wasn't I protected for instance? On the one hand it had been difficult to deal with the fact that she kept us in such an abusive environment, yet on the other, I was feeling bad in a way for her. Although I now saw her as a victim also, I still believe that bottom-line, she was the adult and dropped the ball when she should have got us free of that environment. I realised that I was still pitying and feeling sorry for her. I knew how painful this was for her to hear, but I felt it needed to be said. Why was I and my siblings treated with such violence? Why were we degraded, demeaned and humiliated? Why did you keep us there? I told her I wished she'd have left him; that I was terrified of him. I told her the effect it has all had on me. I told her I needed to know whether or not she cared about me then and also about what I'm going through now. She said she did, and she does. Several days later, I called again. Once again, I get my mother as father was not home. This time we discussed it all for forty five minutes. She finally seemed like she had lifted her head out of the sands of denial as we discussed it openly. It was obvious she was very uncomfortable talking about it and I can't blame her, but to her credit she did. Once again I said I needed to talk with my father and that I would call back. I did call back a few days later and yet again, it is my mother on the phone. "He is not here." She answered. I asked her if she'd told him what I wanted to talk to him about and she tells me she did; only this time there is a wall up. It became immediately evident that her head is back in the sand and she is in full denial once again. She is definitely not going to deal with this. How could this be? She told me she cared about me. After this conversation I felt emotionally gutted. I felt empty and abandoned by her, again.

I wandered down the field and out on to my little lookout point where I love to go and look out at the mountain and watch the hawks circling late in the day overhead, much like the way I used to sit and get lost watching the seabirds for hours and hours as a child. I lay down out there, eventually crying myself to sleep. I don't know exactly how long I slept there, but long enough to awake to pitch darkness. I began walking back to the house with great difficulty as I felt that all of my strength and energy had been sapped from me. It was then that I saw the headlights of the car coming up the field towards me, realising that my husband had been looking for me and was now panicked. We lay out on that grass talking for a long time. How fortunate I have been to have such a man who loves, understands and supports me like this.

Along-with rediscovering my doll from time-to-time, I would also come across a lot of my father's writings which he'd given to me over the years. I had thought I'd got rid of all of them years ago, however recently I kept stumbling across more. All-in-all I found over sixty short stories and poems; many of which droned on about his various dalliances and affairs with other women and also about how wronged he'd been by the world and other nonsensical subjects he'd written about, oftentimes in drunken states. The discovery of these writings had even more of a negative impact on me than periodically rediscovering the doll. So yet again I told myself, they have to go. It would be another couple of weeks before I finally had my burning ceremony. My husband lit the bonfire and stood there with one hand on the shovel lest any escape and his other arm around me as I, page-by-page, threw each one into the flames, along-with them I was voicing out loud what I thought of my father, and when I couldn't think of strong enough words, my husband helped me out. A few minutes into it I began to cry as with each page I would think how not only myself, but my siblings had suffered. I would dedicate with each page these thoughts to each one of my siblings, including myself, feeling that pain anew. I cried for us all. The outcome of this was once again a sense of an enormous burden being lifted from me, and in its place a renewed strength, determination and knowledge that not only I could, but I would confront my father. I had confidence that when it did happen it would be the best timing and I would do it calmly. My opportunity finally came just a few days later.

After six previous attempts of either not getting answers or getting my mother on the phone instead, it finally happened. I heard my father's voice, and strangely enough, it did not invoke the fear it always had. This I knew was a test that told me, "Yes, I really am a little stronger." So how do I start this conversation I've dreamt of having for so many decades? I didn't know where to begin. Eventually I decided to start where I'd tried to two years prior by asking him whether or not he remembered me asking these two questions: "Do you ever think about how your alcoholism has affected the entire family?" and if so, "Do you feel bad about it?" He said that he remembered these questions all too well. I said that I perhaps went about that all wrong, as that was about what he thought, but now I needed to tell him what I thought, and he needed to hear it. It did not go that well in some regards, but then again, I didn't really have any preconceived ideas, nor expectations beforehand; my main goal being to somehow keep him on the phone long enough to tell him very briefly what I thought and felt.

When asked, he said my mother had told him a little of what I wanted to say to him. Therefore, he was prepared by telling me that he was going to make up a long list of all of the good things he had done for me and my siblings as he claimed, 'he remembered everything'. I said that I wished I could remember a long list of good things, but unfortunately the very long list of bad far outweighs that. Even though it took six telephone calls to finally get him, I think the timing was just right as one of my cousins was there which I am convinced kept him from screaming and yelling at me and slamming the phone down right away. I did not plan what I was going to say ahead of time, deciding to just flow with it. I told him how I was absolutely terrified of him as a child; that I dreaded him coming home and I could never understand why he so violently abused me. I was not at all prepared for what I heard next. He began by saying, "Well, you try to raise six children when the working situation was how it was", at which point he then went off further into a tangent about his treatment and the unfairness of the structure of the workplace and all the stress which that brought, etc. I could not believe my ears. I was thinking to myself, "Is this an admission? Why is he making excuses?" I couldn't stand it any longer, so I finally said: "And this is your excuse for beating the hell out of your children? I was an innocent little girl, yet you treated me like I had no value, like I was literally nothing." I told him he was a bully, especially to his children. I told him that it has affected us all in different ways. Peppered all throughout, he kept repeating over and over again the words, "nonsense" and "rubbish" and others not worth mentioning.

Even though I kept reminding myself that I had nothing to convince him of and to just tell him what I feel and think, I did decide to use a few examples of his abuse and I purposely chose those involving only my brothers thinking he wouldn't dare to call us all liars. I reminded him of the intense verbal abuse and humiliation as well. The example I chose to use here was of my little brothers, who were only primary school age, having to stand facing the wall with their pants pulled down exposing their backsides and made to stand on one leg whilst my drunken father taunted them in the presence of his drinking 'friends'. Needless to say, he got quite hostile, denying it vehemently. I told him I was sorry that he chose 'not to remember', but not only did it happen, but my brothers as adults have sobbed over it still, along-with countless other memories. I suggested then that he perhaps talk to them about it and get their version. He said he would not. The examples could have gone on seemingly forever, except for the fact that I kept reminding myself that he will slam the phone down at any moment. Again I reiterated just how profoundly his treatment not only affected me, but also my siblings very deeply. He said that if I wanted to make my life miserable by dwelling on the past, then I could, but we (I presume he meant my mother as well) have moved well on beyond that (another admission perhaps). I told him that I have waited my whole life for an apology; for him to say a heartfelt 'sorry'. He said, "I WILL NOT SAY IT!!" He refused to listen to anymore and slammed the phone down.

Although this was an historic moment for me, my reaction to this conversation with my father was in stark contrast to that of the one with my mother. First of all, I was surprised that I was not shaken up after this. I sat there calmly; taking my time experiencing a strange, yet interesting mixture of emotions and thoughts; for instance, "Well, that's that then." "It's over." "I finally did it, and I can hardly believe it." I felt a sense of complete indifference toward him. Perhaps I had still been hanging on to the notion that there might be some tiny wee speck of remorse in him, but now I had absolutely no doubt whatsoever in my mind at all that he held none. He well and truly did not care one iota about me. Although normally an extremely sad thought, I also realised at the same time that my father no longer had any hold over me now. A great burden had lifted. He had gone; the fear had gone; completely gone. I had lost nothing, but I gained a strength I never thought possible. The tide has finally turned. I could let it go now.

Mira S. Hall

11

I HAVE RIGHTS TOO

Eight years before I was born the United Nations General Assembly adopted and proclaimed the Universal Declaration of Human Rights. In Article 5 it says, "No one shall be subjected to torture or to cruel, inhuman or degrading treatment or punishment". I have been subjected to all of these. As a child verbal and physical abuse was a way of life for me. As an older child I was repeatedly forced into a car; held against my will (nothing short of kidnapping), locked in rooms to be raped and beaten. Nobody was there to enforce these rights, despite pleas for help. I had no voice. I was one of the fortunate ones, however, who still had enough fight in me to not give up until I was free of that hell. I worked hard toward and eventually realising that freedom I'd always dreamt of, and so desperately needed. I subsequently went on to live, enjoy and appreciate a new life for over three decades in peace, freedom and security in my adopted country with my own family. I was content.

Nothing could have prepared me for the complete shock at having my rights violated after all these decades yet again, and the ensuing impact this was to have on my life. My whole adult life I guarded and protected myself by not putting myself in what would normally be considered 'high risk' environments, therefore, to have my rights taken from me in a doctor's office of all places; a place where one should feel and be safe; a place where one should be able to trust; a place where one should be respected. To have this right violated by being subjected to such degrading treatment is despicable to the highest degree. To see someone purport himself as a man of honour, a dedicated doctor whose very profession is to show respect, caring and help to patients, yet behave in a completely opposite manner is totally abhorrent. This kind of unconscionable behaviour should be condemned to the fullest degree. I have a voice now and I will do everything I possibly can to stand up for not only mine, but the rights of all other women, and children. Human rights are there to be protected and enforced. Anything less should NEVER be tolerated.

It was not until this assault as an older woman, which resulted in not only my world coming crashing down around me, but the lid being blown completely off that Pandora's box, my childhood, that I came to realise that I had not dealt fully with my past. The techniques I'd used in the past such as just burying it all deep down as much as possible, just did not work anymore. This situation haunted and tormented me for a year and a half. I became very depressed and withdrawn and sleeping became extremely challenging. The memories, the nightmares all over again made life very difficult. This assault had triggered flashbacks from my past, which obviously exacerbated the emotional pain and suffering. The feelings of despair, hopelessness and pain returned. Oh, the pain! And oh, so fresh.

Out of desperation I finally took the suggestion of my daughter and sought out a therapist, something I'd always thought of as a weakness. I had always handled everything on my own and had shared only parts of my past with only a very select few, so the thought of going to a complete stranger for help was not only foreign to me, but extremely daunting. I did not understand what was happening to me. As it happened this angel of a therapist had a quarter of a century's worth of experience working with victims of abuse. It was here that I was first told that I was clearly suffering from Post-traumatic Stress Disorder. This was all very new for me.

The only thing I knew about it was that it was something soldiers sometimes suffered with when returning from a battlefield. This was a very long, exhausting, laborious, but oftentimes, enlightening process. As I stared down my past head on, I became stronger and stronger, eventually finding my voice.

As for that so-called doctor; well, first of all, he did not deserve such a title. He was an utter disgrace and betrayal, not only to his profession, but as a human being. I had a voice now and I did stand up, and I did speak out, loud and clear, and along-with the help and support of many other voices, I made sure that privilege was taken from him.

It's Okay Sweetie…. One Day You'll Fly Far, Far Away…..

12

DARE I SAY …..PRIDE

Surviving an abusive childhood can be a miracle in itself. Once I'd realized that I had actually come out of it physically intact, I had to set about putting as much distance between myself and my abusers as possible. For me personally, that meant moving to another hemisphere. Deep in my soul I knew it couldn't work any other way. I had to give myself the greatest fighting chance possible. In retrospect, this was for me personally, the best thing I could ever have done for myself.

Although painfully shy, I believe I always was a fighter. Somehow I think I always knew that I didn't deserve to be treated the way I had been; nobody did. I made a solemn vow to myself as an older child, that no-one would ever, ever abuse me again. As I then began my 'post-abuse journey', it struck me very clearly that my life's decisions, as far as what path I took, from where on this world I decided to make my home, and with whom, were all my choices; MY CHOICES!! It was as if my eyes had been opened and the whole world was in front of me, and quite literally, it was. I was being given a second chance; a fresh start. This was quite overwhelming, but in all the right ways. I was not afraid of going down the wrong path. I knew I wasn't going to squander this gift; freedom.

Now I find myself decades further on in this journey and I can't help but reflect on the fact of just how much I have been blessed with a wonderfully loving husband who has shown me nothing but respect, always. I was given the gift of children and grandchildren. I loved being a mother, raising my children to never doubt that they were safe, unconditionally loved, and respected. I now knew what it was like to live safely in the knowledge that I would not be abused in my home. My old life seemed worlds away. As an adult I had dealt with my past the best way that I knew how; by choosing to keep it in my past, or so I thought. I tried very hard not to dwell on it, instead being always grateful for where my life had taken me. It was not always easy. It took many years for the nightmares to retreat. The memories, with all their ugliness would rear their heads of course from time-to-time. However, I'd come to believe that I was 'strong', at least stronger than they were. It helped tremendously being thankful for what I now had, and how far I'd come. For decades I chose not to allow my abusive childhood to define my life, or excuse it in any way.

Little-by-little, step-by-careful-step, I began confronting that past, as best as I could. It would be horrendously painful at times, and the progress slower than I would have liked. I continued to question every now and again just how much this process could be 'keeping it alive' as I wanted so very badly to forget it all; move on once and for all, never to revisit it again. Realistically, I know that the memories cannot be erased. Oh how wonderfully easy it would be if we could just click that delete button on selective memories just like a computer. Accepting that I'll always have those memories has been difficult. The pain revisits, but not quite as often now. I know that ever-so-slowly those wounds have been healing. One thing though that I had not allowed myself, and that was to feel proud about myself, much less express it. Perhaps, now it is time to allow myself this luxury, so here goes:

I am proud that I got myself out of the abuse
I am proud that I chose the right path in life; statistics were most definitely not on my side

I am proud that I kept my vow; never to choose to allow abuse again

I am proud that I confronted my abusers; at least those still living

I am proud that I have been a good mother

I am proud that I have had a good marriage

I am proud that I want and strive to be a better person

I am proud that I care about people

I had no physical awards to show or feel proud of in my old life, but now deep in my soul, this new and unfamiliar feeling stirs.... PRIDE! I'm claiming it. I'm keeping it. I've earned it!!

It's Okay Sweetie.... One Day You'll Fly Far, Far Away.....

13

AFTERWORD

I do not profess to be an expert on the subjects of child abuse, nor sexual abuse by any means. No, I will leave that to the professionals. However, as a survivor of both, all I can do is share my story in the hopes that it may somehow help, or possibly even inspire others by showing them that survival is possible and dreams are most definitely worth having.

Sadly, my story of abuse is not unique at all; no, it is all too common in fact. Tens of thousands of innocent children are subjected to some form of abuse every single day in the United States alone. This is well beyond a national shame. I have learnt not only that I matter, but every single person matters and has the right to be safe. There are a myriad of stories to be told. I know I cannot change the world, but perhaps I can make a difference in one person's life, who in turn can make a difference in the next, and one-by-one we can make a change. There are many heroes out there; mostly unsung, who are working tirelessly to make a significant difference to this very prevalent affliction embedded deep within our society. Unfortunately, this issue is far too often ignored. There is no community where this secret shame does not exist. The insidiously poisonous effects of abuse infiltrate shockingly throughout every single sector of our society. It knows no boundaries whatsoever; be it racial, age or socio-economic. It is more than a family problem; this is a societal challenge, the effects of which are far-reaching and the consequences long-lasting, and oftentimes, life-long, and far too often, reaching down to generation after generation.

It is my utmost hope that first and foremost my story will speak to victims by helping them to see that not only is there always hope, but also just how very important it is to dream and work toward those dreams and goals and above all else, never, never, NEVER give up!! You don't have to be victims anymore. It doesn't have to be a life-long sentence. You too can be a survivor. There is help out there. Keep speaking out and keep asking until you find the help you need. Don't let embarrassment, shame or fear prevent you from this. I did this for far too long.

Secondly, I would like to help in bringing more public awareness to this very urgent issue to those who can help, who can make a difference. The floodlights need to be shone much more brightly upon this issue which is beyond epidemic proportions. There are millions upon millions of confirmed cases each year of child abuse in the United States alone. By speaking up, many victims realise that this can attract judgement and unwanted attention. Oftentimes these victims become victimized all over again. Together we can make a difference by exposing as many of these well-kept, dark secrets as possible. Because of the secrecy, denial and stigma surrounding this very serious and ugly issue, most cases do not even get reported. Very sadly this means leaving millions of children, particularly those living in alcoholic and other substance users' homes unidentified.

Although significant progress has been made, much more education needs to be provided for all ages. Children and youth need easier access to self-help and support groups, especially for the victims, but also for survivors. As a society, we cannot afford for any of these programmes to be cut. Great strides have been made in educating those who work with children, for example, teachers, coaches, hospitals and other healthcare providers to name just a few. This needs to continue much more vigilantly. I firmly believe that if such education programmes were available and in place when I was growing up I would not have fallen through the cracks as easily, particularly when I did at one point go and tell a doctor. Perhaps you can lend your voice and speak up for those who don't have one. This could literally mean the difference between life and death for an innocent child. Perhaps it is support and encouragement when you know circumstances are difficult. You can make a difference; we all can. As a society this needs to become a part of our collective conscience.

RESOURCES

For resources and information on how you can help in the efforts of prevention and/or find out about treatment programmes on Child Abuse, or Adult Survivors of Child Abuse, the following organisations may be helpful:

PCA America National Office:
www.preventchildabuse.org

Prevent Child Abuse America
228 South Wabash Avenue
10th Floor
Chicago, IL. 60604

U.S. Department of Health and Human Services
www.hhs.gov
Administration for Children and Families
Will provide State toll-free numbers for specific agencies designated to receive and investigate reports of suspected child abuse and neglect.

(ASCA) Adult Survivors of Child Abuse
P.O. Box 14477
San Francisco, CA. 94114
www.ascasupport.org
phone: (415-928-4576

ASCA is an International self-help support group programme designed specifically for adult survivors of neglect, physical, sexual and/or emotional abuse.

(OCAN) The Office on Child Abuse and Neglect with the
Children's Bureau coordinate Child Abuse Prevention Month
activities at the Federal level, providing information and releasing
updated national statistics.

In 1983 April was proclaimed as the first National Child Abuse
Prevention Month. This information can be found at:
www.childwelfare.gov along with information on not only
prevention but also responding to child abuse. There are many
resources here not only for professionals, but the general public.

Phone: 1-800-394-3366

**(CAPTA) Child Abuse Prevention and Treatment Act passed
legislation in 1974**.

In the 1980's the U.S. Senate and House of Representatives
resolved that the week of 6th-12th June, 1982 was designated as the
first National Child Abuse Prevention Week.

ABOUT THE AUTHOR

Mira Hall was born and raised in New Zealand. After living for a short time in England she immigrated to the United States where she has been fortunate enough to experience living in such places as the Rocky Mountains, California's Central Valley, the San Fernando Valley and the Mojave Desert. She has two grown children. She currently resides in rural Pennsylvania with her husband where she enjoys writing, gardening, grandchildren and the peace and simplicity of country life.

Contact: itsokay@ptd.net